elevate science

SAVVAS
LEARNING COMPANY

You are an author!

This is your book to keep. Write and draw in it! Record your data and discoveries in it! You are an author of this book!

Print your name, school, town, and state below.

My Photo

Name_____

School _____

Town, State_____

ISBN-13: 978-0-328-92509-4
ISBN-10: 0-328-92509-8

9 21

Program Authors

ZIPPORAH MILLER, EdD
Coordinator for K-12 Science Programs, Anne Arundel County Public Schools.
Zipporah Miller currently serves as the Senior Manager for Organizational Learning with the Anne Arundel County Public School System. Prior to that she served as the K-12 Coordinator for science in Anne Arundel County. She conducts national training to science stakeholders on the Next Generation Science Standards. Dr. Miller also served as the Associate Executive Director for Professional Development Programs and conferences at the National Science Teachers Association (NSTA) and served as a reviewer during the development of Next Generation Science Standards. Dr. Miller holds a doctoral degree from University of Maryland College Park, a master's degree in school administration and supervision from Bowie State University, and a bachelor's degree from Chadron State College.

MICHAEL J. PADILLA, PhD
Professor Emeritus, Eugene P. Moore School of Education, Clemson University, Clemson, South Carolina
Michael J. Padilla taught science in middle and secondary schools, has more than 30 years of experience educating middle grades science teachers, and served as one of the writers of the 1996 U.S. National Science Education Standards. In recent years Mike has focused on teaching science to English Language Learners. His extensive leadership experience, serving as Principal Investigator on numerous National Science Foundation and U.S. Department of Education grants, resulted in more than $35 million in funding to improve science education. He served as president of the National Science Teachers Association, the world's largest science teaching organization, in 2005–6.

MICHAEL E. WYSESSION, PhD
Professor of Earth and Planetary Sciences, Washington University, St. Louis, Missouri
An author on more than 100 science and science education publications, Dr. Wysession was awarded the prestigious National Science Foundation Presidential Faculty Fellowship and Packard Foundation Fellowship for his research in geophysics, primarily focused on using seismic tomography to determine the forces driving plate tectonics. Dr. Wysession is also a leader in geoscience literacy and education, including being chair of the Earth Science Literacy Principles, author of several popular geology Great Courses video lecture series, and a lead writer of the Next Generation Science Standards*.

Program Consultants

Carol Baker
Science Curriculum

Dr. Carol K. Baker is superintendent for Lyons Elementary K-8 School District in Lyons, Illinois. Prior to that, she was Director of Curriculum for Science and Music in Oak Lawn, Illinois. Before that she taught Physics and Earth Science for 18 years. In the recent past, Dr. Baker also wrote assessment questions for ACT (EXPLORE and PLAN), was elected president of the Illinois Science Teachers Association from 2011-2013 and served as a member of the Museum of Science and Industry advisory boards in Chicago. She is a writer of the Next Generation Science Standards. Dr. Baker received her BS in Physics and a science teaching certification. She completed her Master of Educational Administration (K-12) and earned her doctorate in Educational Leadership.

Jim Cummins
ELL

Dr. Cummins's research focuses on literacy development in multilingual schools and the role technology plays in learning across the curriculum. *Elevate Science* incorporates research-based principles for integrating language with the teaching of academic content based on Dr. Cummins's work.

Elfrieda Hiebert
Literacy

Dr. Hiebert is the President and CEO of TextProject, a nonprofit aimed at providing open-access resources for instruction of beginning and struggling readers, and a former primary school teacher. She is also a research associate at the University of California Santa Cruz. Her research addresses how fluency, vocabulary, and knowledge can be fostered through appropriate texts, and her contributions have been recognized through awards, such as the Oscar Causey Award for Outstanding Contributions to Reading Research (Literacy Research Association, 2015), Research to Practice Award (American Educational Research Association, 2013), William S. Gray Citation of Merit Award for Outstanding Contributions to Reading Research (International Reading Association, 2008).

Content Reviewers

Alex Blom, Ph.D.
Associate Professor
Department Of Physical Sciences
Alverno College
Milwaukee, Wisconsin

Joy Branlund, Ph.D.
Department of Physical Science
Southwestern Illinois College
Granite City, Illinois

Judy Calhoun
Associate Professor
Physical Sciences
Alverno College
Milwaukee, Wisconsin

Stefan Debbert
Associate Professor of Chemistry
Lawrence University
Appleton, Wisconsin

Diane Doser
Professor
Department of Geological Sciences
University of Texas at El Paso
El Paso, Texas

Rick Duhrkopf, Ph. D.
Department of Biology
Baylor University
Waco, Texas

Jennifer Liang
University Of Minnesota Duluth
Duluth, Minnesota

Heather Mernitz, Ph.D.
Associate Professor of Physical Sciences
Alverno College
Milwaukee, Wisconsin

Joseph McCullough, Ph.D.
Cabrillo College
Aptos, California

Katie M. Nemeth, Ph.D.
Assistant Professor
College of Science and Engineering
University of Minnesota Duluth
Duluth, Minnesota

Maik Pertermann
Department of Geology
Western Wyoming Community College
Rock Springs, Wyoming

Scott Rochette
Department of the Earth Sciences
The College at Brockport
State University of New York
Brockport, New York

David Schuster
Washington University in St Louis
St. Louis, Missouri

Shannon Stevenson
Department of Biology
University of Minnesota Duluth
Duluth, Minnesota

Paul Stoddard, Ph.D.
Department of Geology and Environmental Geosciences
Northern Illinois University
DeKalb, Illinois

Nancy Taylor
American Public University
Charles Town, West Virginia

Safety Reviewers

Douglas Mandt, M.S.
Science Education Consultant
Edgewood, Washington

Juliana Textley, Ph.D.
Author, NSTA books on school science safety
Adjunct Professor
Lesley University
Cambridge, Massachusetts

Teacher Reviewers

Jennifer Bennett, M.A.
Memorial Middle School
Tampa, Florida

Sonia Blackstone
Lake County Schools
Howey In the Hills, Florida

Teresa Bode
Roosevelt Elementary
Tampa, Florida

Tyler C. Britt, Ed.S.
Curriculum & Instructional
 Practice Coordinator
Raytown Quality Schools
Raytown, Missouri

A. Colleen Campos
Grandview High School
Aurora, Colorado

Coleen Doulk
Challenger School
Spring Hill, Florida

Mary D. Dube
Burnett Middle School
Seffner, Florida

Sandra Galpin
Adams Middle School
Tampa, Florida

Margaret Henry
Lebanon Junior High School
Lebanon, Ohio

Christina Hill
Beth Shields Middle School
Ruskin, Florida

Judy Johnis
Gorden Burnett Middle School
Seffner, Florida

Karen Y. Johnson
Beth Shields Middle School
Ruskin, Florida

Jane Kemp
Lockhart Elementary School
Tampa, Florida

Denise Kuhling
Adams Middle School
Tampa, Florida

Esther Leonard M.Ed. and L.M.T.
Gifted and Talented Implementation Specialist
San Antonio Independent School District
San Antonio, Texas

Kelly Maharaj
Science Department Chairperson
Challenger K8 School of Science and
 Mathematics
Elgin, Florida

Kevin J. Maser, Ed.D.
H. Frank Carey Jr/Sr High School
Franklin Square, New York

Angie L. Matamoros, Ph.D.
ALM Science Consultant
Weston, Florida

Corey Mayle
Brogden Middle School
Durham, North Carolina

Keith McCarthy
George Washington Middle School
Wayne, New Jersey

Yolanda O. Peña
John F. Kennedy Junior High School
West Valley City, Utah

Kathleen M. Poe
Jacksonville Beach Elementary School
Jacksonville Beach, Florida

Wendy Rauld
Monroe Middle School
Tampa, Florida

Bryna Selig
Gaithersburg Middle School
Gaithersburg, Maryland

Pat (Patricia) Shane, Ph.D.
STEM & ELA Education Consultant
Chapel Hill, North Carolina

Diana Shelton
Burnett Middle School
Seffner, Florida

Nakia Sturrup
Jennings Middle School
Seffner, Florida

Melissa Triebwasser
Walden Lake Elementary
Plant City, Florida

Michele Bubley Wiehagen
Science Coach
Miles Elementary School
Tampa, Florida

Pauline Wilcox
Instructional Science Coach
Fox Chapel Middle School
Spring Hill, Florida

Pushes and Pulls

Quest

In this Quest activity, you meet a sail designer. She needs your help. She wants you to find the best shape to use for a sail. You will design the sail for a sail car.

Like the sail designer, you will complete activities and labs. You will use what you learn in the lessons to make your sail. Then you will use it to race a car.

Find your Quest activities on pages 11, 16, and 26.

Career Connection Sail Designer on page 29

- ▶ VIDEO
- 📖 eTEXT
- 👆 INTERACTIVITY
- ▶ SCIENCE SONG
- 🎮 GAME
- 📄 DOCUMENT
- ☑ ASSESSMENT

HANDS-ON LAB

Topic 2

K-2-ETS1-1, K-2-ETS1-2, K-2-ETS1-3

Matter

Quest

In this Quest activity, you meet a science teacher. She needs your help to sort objects.

Like the science teacher, you will complete activities and labs. You will use what you learn in the lessons to sort objects. Then you will use tools to put the objects away.

Find your Quest activities on pages 47, 54, and 60

Career Connection Science Teacher on page 65

- ▶ VIDEO
- 📖 eTEXT
- 👆 INTERACTIVITY
- ▶ SCIENCE SONG
- 🎮 GAME
- 📄 DOCUMENT
- ☑ ASSESSMENT

The Essential Question

HANDS-ON LAB

Topic 3

Sunlight

Quest

In this Quest activity, you meet an architect. He needs your help. He wants to build a doghouse. The doghouse should keep his dog cool on sunny days.

Like the architect, you will complete activities and labs. You will use what you learn in the lessons to plan and design a doghouse. Then you can build it.

Find your Quest activities on pages 82 and 92.

Career Connection Architect on page 95

▶	VIDEO
📖	eTEXT
👆	INTERACTIVITY
▶	SCIENCE SONG
🎮	GAME
📄	DOCUMENT
☑	ASSESSMENT

HANDS-ON LAB

Topic 4

Earth's Weather

K-ESS2-1, K-ESS3-2, K-ESS3-3, K-2-ETS1-1, K-2-ETS1-2, K-2-ETS1-3

- ▶ VIDEO
- 📖 eTEXT
- 👆 INTERACTIVITY
- ▶ SCIENCE SONG
- 🎮 GAME
- 📄 DOCUMENT
- ✓ ASSESSMENT

Quest

In this Quest activity, you meet a storm chaser. She needs your help. She wants to make a safety poster. It will tell people how to stay safe in storms.

Like a storm chaser, you will complete activities and labs. You will use what you learn in the lessons to make a safety poster. You will help people stay safe in storms.

Find your Quest activities on pages 113, 121, 126, and 134.

Career Connection Storm Chaser on page 137

The Essential Question

HANDS-ON LAB

Topic 5

Needs of Living Things

K-LS1-1, K-2-ETS1-1, K-2-ETS1-2

Quest

In this Quest activity, you meet a wildlife biologist. She needs your help. She wants to make a book about a new park. It will show people what plants and animals need to live in the park.

Like a wildlife biologist, you will complete activities and labs. You will use what you learn in the lessons to draw a picture of the park. You will include what the living things need.

Find your Quest activities on pages 155, 161, 168, and 176.

Career Connection Wildlife Biologist on page 179

 VIDEO

 eTEXT

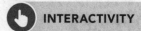 INTERACTIVITY

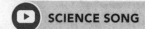 SCIENCE SONG

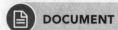 GAME

 DOCUMENT

ASSESSMENT

The Essential Question

HANDS-ON LAB

Environments

Quest

In this Quest activity, you meet a park ranger. He needs your help. He wants to make signs for a nature trail. The signs will tell people how to use the trail wisely.

Like a park ranger, you will complete activities and labs. You will use what you learn in the lessons to make trail signs. The signs will help plants and animals along the trail.

Find your Quest activities on pages 197, 203, 208, and 216.

Career Connection Park Ranger on page 221

 ▶ VIDEO

 📖 eTEXT

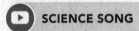 👆 INTERACTIVITY

 ▶ SCIENCE SONG

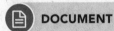 🎮 GAME

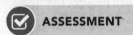 📄 DOCUMENT

☑ ASSESSMENT

HANDS-ON LAB

Elevate your thinking!

Elevate Science takes science to a whole new level and lets you take ownership of your learning. Explore science in the world around you. Investigate how things work. Think critically and solve problems! *Elevate Science* helps you think like a scientist, so you're ready for a world of discoveries.

Explore Your World

Explore real-life scenarios with engaging Quests that dig into science topics around the world. You can:

- Solve real-world problems
- Apply skills and knowledge
- Communicate solutions

Quest Kickoff

Find the Parents

What clues help us find a young animal's parent?

Make Connections

Elevate Science connects science to other subjects and shows you how to better understand the world through:

- Mathematics
- Reading and Writing
- Literacy

Literacy ▸ Toolbox

Main Ideas and Details All living things grow and change is the main idea. Use the details to tell how a watermelon plant changes during its life cycle.

Math ▸ Toolbox

Compare Numbers You can compare how long objects are. Parent rabbits have longer ears than young rabbits. Use cubes to measure the lengths of two classroom objects. Which is longer?

Connecting Concepts ▸ Toolbox

Patterns Nature has many patterns. A **pattern** is something that repeats. Parents protect their young. They use their bodies to protect them. What patterns do you see on these two pages?

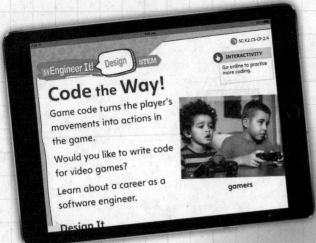

Build Skills for the Future

- Master the Engineering Design Process
- Apply critical thinking and analytical skills
- Learn about STEM careers

Focus on Reading Skills

Elevate Science creates ongoing reading connections to help you develop the reading skills you need to succeed. Features include:

- Leveled Readers
- Literacy Connection Features
- Reading Checks

Main Idea and Details

Nature scientists observe animals. Read about the main idea and details of geese and their young.

The main idea is what the sentences are about. Details tell about the main idea.

GAME
Practice what you learn with the Toolbox Games.

Enter the Lab

Hands-on experiments and virtual labs help you test ideas and show what you know in performance-based assessments. Scaffolded labs include:

- STEM Labs
- Design Your Own
- Open-ended Labs

Alike and Different: Living Things

Click the pictures. Compare how living things and their parents are alike and different. Write your answer below.

Type your answer here.

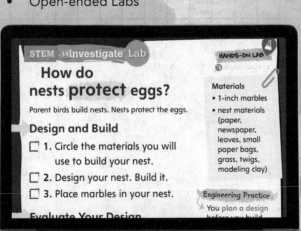

STEM uInvestigate Lab

HANDS-ON LAB

How do nests **protect** eggs?

Parent birds build nests. Nests protect the eggs.

Design and Build

☐ 1. Circle the materials you will use to build your nest.

☐ 2. Design your nest. Build it.

☐ 3. Place marbles in your nest.

Evaluate Your Design

Materials
- 1-inch marbles
- nest materials (paper, newspaper, leaves, small paper bags, grass, twigs, modeling clay)

Engineering Practice
You plan a design before you build

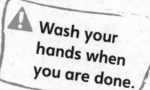

Engineering Practice
You **plan a design** before you build something.

⚠ **Wash your hands when you are done.**

Pushes and Pulls

Next Generation Science Standards

K-PS2-1. Plan and conduct an investigation to compare the effects of different strengths or different directions of pushes and pulls on the motion of an object.

K-PS2-2. Analyze data to determine if a design solution works as intended to change the speed or direction of an object with a push or a pull.

K-2-ETS1-3. Analyze data from tests of two objects designed to solve the same problem to compare the strengths and weaknesses of how each performs.

The Essential Question What happens if you push or pull an object?

Show What You Know

Put a box around a pull.

Wind Makes It Go

How can we use wind to push or pull something?

Phenomenon Hi, I'm Ms. Alvarez! I'm a sail designer. I think of ways to make sails to help things go faster. I need your help.

My friend wants to win a sail car race. Help me find the best shape for a sail for his car. It should help his car go fast in a big wind.

Follow the path. Do the steps to make your sail. Check off each one with **QUEST CHECK ✓ OFF** .

Next Generation Science Standards

K-PS2-1. Plan and conduct an investigation to compare the effects of different strengths or different directions of pushes and pulls on the motion of an object.

K-PS2-2 Analyze data to determine if a design solution works as intended to change the speed or direction of an object with a push or a pull.

K-2-ETS1-3 Analyze data from tests of two objects designed to solve the same problem to compare the strengths and weaknesses of how each performs.

Quest Check-In Lab 2

Lesson 2 ●

Use what you learned to tell what happens when you blow on your sail.

Quest Check-In Lab 3

Lesson 3 ◆

Use what you learned to make the best sail.

Quest Check-In 1

Lesson 1 ■

Use what you learned to draw a sail for your car.

FINISH

Quest Findings

Complete your Quest. What is a fun way to find the best sail shape?

START

How do things *move*?

Car designers observe how cars move.
They ask questions.
How can you move things?

Materials
- 4 classroom objects

Procedure

☐ **1.** Choose 4 objects.

☐ **2.** Think of ways to move each object.

☐ **3.** Move each object.

☐ **4.** Draw one object in the box.

Use arrows to show how the object moves.

Science Practice

You **plan and conduct** an investigation to tell others what you learned.

Analyze and Interpret Data

5. Which object did you move?

_____

_____

Cause and Effect

Car designers understand cause and effect. Read about what causes a bicycle to move.

 GAME
Practice what you learn with the Mini Games.

A cause makes something happen.

An effect is what happens.

My Bike

I have a bike.

I can push the pedals quickly.

My bike goes fast.

I can push the pedals gently.

My bike goes slowly.

☑ **READING CHECK** Cause and Effect

Circle a cause. Underline an effect.

Lesson 1

Pushes and Pulls

 **VIDEO**

Watch a video about pushes and pulls.

Vocabulary

push
pull

I can observe how objects move.

K-PS2-1

Jumpstart Discovery!

How are the dogs moving the toy?

How can you move something?

How can we make objects move?

Can you make objects move?
Try it and observe what happens.

Procedure

☐ **1.** Think of ways to make the objects move.

☐ **2. Observe** where the objects go.

☐ **3. Show** where it goes.

Analyze and Interpret Data

4. Explain. How did the objects move?

_____

- - - - - - - - - - - - - - - -

_____

_____

_____

_____

_____

Suggested Materials

- pencil
- marker
- eraser
- book
- wood block

Science Practice

You **analyze data** from tests to tell if it works as you thought.

Pushes and Pulls

You can **push** an object to move it away from you.

You can **pull** an object to move it toward you.

☑ **Reading Check** **Cause and Effect**
Underline the two words that make an object move.

Tell about the picture.

Does it show a push?

Does it show a pull?

Identify Write push or pull for each part of the picture.

Engineering ▸ Toolbox

Conduct an Investigation Stand blocks in a path.

Push the first one.

Tell what happens.

Quest Connection

Tell how a push or pull can make something move.

Ways Objects Move

A push or pull can change the way an object moves.

The ball rolls to the boy.

The boy pushes it with a kick.

The ball moves away from the boy.

Identify Look at each picture. Draw an arrow to show direction.

push

pull

Shapes of Sails

Wind pushes sails of all shapes.

The best shape will get more wind.

Draw a sail for your car.

Talk with a partner.

Tell why your sail shape is best.

Lesson 2

Change in Movement

▶ VIDEO

Watch a video about changes in movement.

Vocabulary

speed
direction

I can observe different ways objects can move.

I can understand why objects move.

K-PS2-1

Jumpstart Discovery!

You are the marble.

Act it out.

Go round and round.

Spin.

How do objects move ?

Tell how objects around you move in different ways.

Materials
- ball
- ruler
- top
- button on a string

Procedure

☐ 1. Think of ways you can move an object.

☐ 2. Test and observe.

☐ 3. Move each object a new way.

Science Practice

You **explain** when you tell how something happens.

Analyze and Interpret Data

4. **Tell** how each object moves.

5. **Tell** a word from the word bank for each object you tested.

fast slow roll spin slide wobble

Different Ways to Move

Objects move in different **directions**.

They can move back and forth.

They can move up and down.

They can move round and round.

INTERACTIVITY

Use the interactivity to answer the question, "How do things move?"

Identify Label how each object is moving.

swing

seesaw

Different Speeds

Objects move at different **speeds**.

Push hard.

A carousel spins fast.

Push softly.

A carousel spins slowly.

Crosscutting Concepts ▸ Toolbox

Cause and Effect
The strength of a push or pull is a cause. How fast or slowly an object moves is the effect. What strength of a push do you need to make a carousel spin fast?

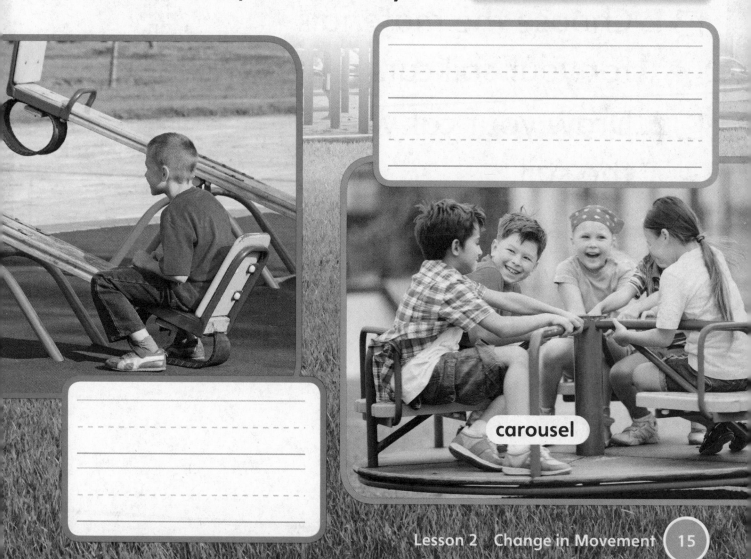

carousel

How can you ⟨build⟩ your sail car?

It is time to make your sail.
Design your sail car.
Build it.
Then test it.

Suggested Materials

- plastic lids, foam pieces
- plastic cups
- paper bake cups
- tissue paper
- toothpicks
- tape
- ruler
- fan

Design and Test

☐ **1.** Choose the materials for your sail car.

☐ **2.** Draw your car with the sail.

☐ **3.** Tell how the sail will push the car.

☐ **4.** Test your sail in the wind.

Engineering Practice

Engineers **test** what they build.

Evaluate Your Solution

5. What worked?

_____

_____

_____

_____

6. What did not work?

_____

_____

_____

_____

7. What would you change?

_____

_____

_____

uEngineer It! Design STEM

VIDEO

Watch a video about engineers designing tools.

Maze Craze!

Phenomenon Have you walked through a maze?

There are a lot of turns.

Design It

Build a maze.

Roll a little ball inside it.

CCC Cause and Effect

What makes the ball change direction?

1. Draw a picture of your maze.

2. Build the maze on a table.

3. Try it out with a ball.

4. Make changes.

5. Have a friend try your maze.

Design It

Which part of your maze did not work?

Tell how you would fix it.

Change Movement with Pushes and Pulls

VIDEO

Watch a video about changes in movement.

Vocabulary

motion

I can investigate how objects move.

K-PS2-2, K-2-ETS1-3

Jumpstart Discovery!

Tell ways that a push can move a ball.

Act them out.

How do you roll?

Scientists study how objects move. How does the strength of a push affect the way an object moves?

Materials
- balls
- tape
- blocks

Procedure

☐ **1.** Work with a partner.

☐ **2.** Make the balls go in a straight line.

☐ **3.** Make the balls change direction.

☐ **4.** Make the balls change speed.

Science Practice

You plan your investigation before you begin.

Analyze and Interpret Data

5. Draw what happens when the balls hit each other.

Objects Change Motion

Use a push or a pull.

Make an object move.

This is its **motion**.

A push or pull can stop its motion.

INTERACTIVITY

Use the interactivity to make a bike travel in different directions.

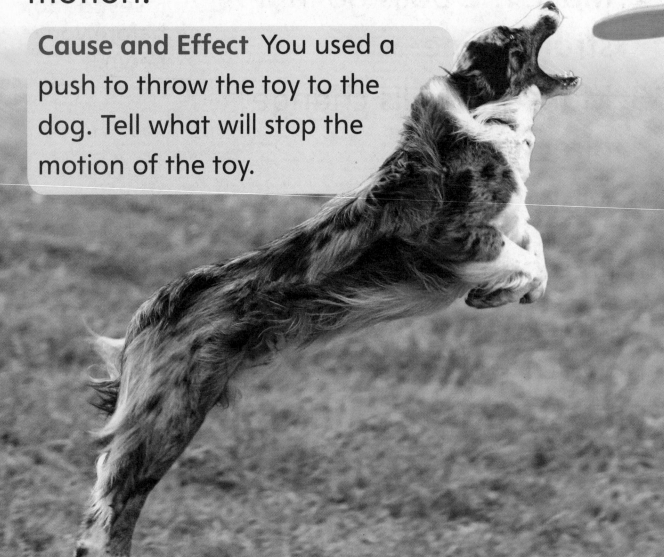

Cause and Effect You used a push to throw the toy to the dog. Tell what will stop the motion of the toy.

How Objects Fall

Some objects bounce when they fall.

Some objects just fall.

They do not bounce back up.

Predict You push the ball off a table.
Will it fall and bounce?
Will it just fall?

Quest Connection

You want to move your sail car.
Tell how you can start its motion.

Direction and Motion

A moving object goes in a direction.

Another object can push or pull it.

The push or pull will change its direction.

Visual Literacy Tell a story about the cars. Draw what happens next.

HANDS-ON LAB

K-PS2-2, K-2-ETS1-3, SEP.4

How does wind move my sail car?

Find out how your sail car works in wind. You may need to change some parts.

Materials

• sail car

• hair dryer or fan

Suggested Materials

• plastic lids, foam pieces

• plastic cups

• paper bake cups

Improve Your Design

☐ 1. Look at your sail car.

☐ 2. Make it better.

☐ 3. Decide what to use for wind.

☐ 4. Get your car to go faster. Get it to change direction.

Engineering Practice

You **test** a design to see if it works.

Evaluate Your Design

5. **Explain** Tell what would make your sail car move faster in the wind.

Add Numbers

The symbol + tells you to add two or more numbers.

Count the red bikes. How many do you see?

Count the blue bikes. How many do you see?

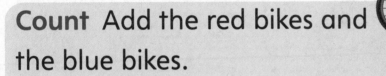

Count Add the red bikes and the blue bikes.

How many bikes do you count?

Red Bikes   Blue Bikes   Red and Blue Bikes

 +  =

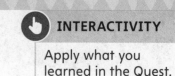
Wind Makes It Go

How can we use wind to move something fast?

Phenomenon Think about the shape of your sail.

Tell why your sail will work the best in a big wind.

Show What You Found

Race your car with your group. Which sail works best? Why?

QUEST CHECK ✓ OFF

Sailboat Designer

This man makes sailboats. He learns about wind and water. He looks at how boats move. His boats are safe for people. They go fast, too!

Write one fact you know about boats.

_____

_____

_____

_____

The Essential Question What happens if you push or pull an object?

Show What You Learned

Tell a partner what you learned about motion.

1. Each photo shows a push or a pull. Fill in the chart. The first one is done for you.

	Push	Pull
	x	

2. How is the ball moving?

   a. up and down

   b. zigzag

   c. curved

   d. back and forth

3. Sam has a toy sailboat.
The wind blows on the sail.
Draw an arrow where the
boat will go.

Read and answer questions 1-4.

Jenna is on a kickball team.

She is the pitcher.

She rolls the kickball to Robert.

She uses a hard push to make the ball go fast.

Robert kicks the ball.

The ball flies up in the air.

Jenna catches it!

Jenna's coach cheers.

1. How did the ball move to Robert?
   a. with a push
   b. with a pull
   c. with a kick
   d. with a bat

2. What kind of push does the pitcher use?

   a. zigzag

   b. hard

   c. soft

   d. up and down

3. Robert kicks the ball. Who stops the ball's motion?

   a. Robert

   b. Jenna

   c. the coach

   d. a fence

4. Jenna rolls the ball to Robert. Draw an arrow to show where the ball will go.

How do objects change their motion?

Phenomenon Objects can move with a push or a pull. Use what you learned to tell how objects move.

Procedure

☐ **1.** Choose an object.

☐ **2.** Make it move.

☐ **3.** Push it while it moves.

☐ **4.** Observe what happens.

☐ **5.** Choose a different object.

☐ **6.** Make a plan to change the motion with a pull.

Suggested Materials

- string
- balls
- crayons
- toy cars
- feathers
- blocks

Science Practice

You **plan and conduct** an investigation to tell others what you learned.

Observations

Object	What Happened

Analyze and Interpret Data

7. **CCC Cause and Effect** Tell what made each object change its motion.

_____

- - - - - - - - - - - - - - - - - -

_____

_____

_____

Matter

Next Generation Science Standards

K-2-ETS1-1 Ask questions, make observations, and gather information about a situation people want to change to define a simple problem that can be solved through the development of a new or improved object or tool.

K-2-ETS1-2 Develop a simple sketch, drawing, or physical model to illustrate how the shape of an object helps it function as needed to solve a given problem.

Go online to access
your digital course.

▶ VIDEO

📖 eTEXT

👆 INTERACTIVITY

▶ SCIENCE SONG

🎮 GAME

☑ ASSESSMENT

The Essential Question How can you classify different objects?

Show What You Know

Circle a soft, red object.

Put a box around a hard, blue object.

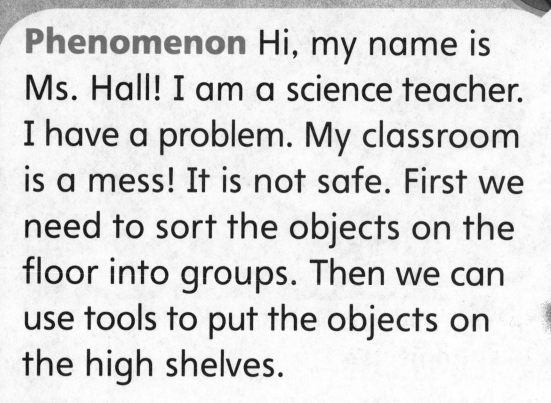

A Messy Classroom

How can we sort objects to put them away safely?

Phenomenon Hi, my name is Ms. Hall! I am a science teacher. I have a problem. My classroom is a mess! It is not safe. First we need to sort the objects on the floor into groups. Then we can use tools to put the objects on the high shelves.

Follow the path. Do the steps to sort the objects. Check off each step here **QUEST CHECK ✓ OFF**.

K-2-ETS1-1 Ask questions, make observations, and gather information about a situation people want to change to define a simple problem that can be solved through the development of a new or improved object or tool.

Quest Check-In Lab 2

Lesson 2 ●

Use what you learned about ways to sort objects.

VIDEO

Watch a video to learn what a science teacher does.

Quest Check-In Lab 3

Lesson 3 ◆

Use what you learned about matter. Sort objects a new way.

Quest Check-In 1

Lesson 1 ■

Use what you learned about senses to compare objects.

Quest Findings

Finish your Quest. Find a fun way to show and tell about your objects.

What is the object?

Scientists observe objects.
How can you use your senses
to ask questions about an object?

Procedure

☐ 1. Hide an object in the bag.

☐ 2. Give the bag to your partner.

☐ 3. Your partner can ask questions to guess the object.

☐ 4. Let your partner have a turn hiding an object in the bag.

Analyze and Interpret Data

5. Tell how you guessed the object.

Materials

- bag
- small classroom objects

Science Practice

You can ask questions to find out about objects.

 Do not taste any materials.

Main Idea and Details

🎮 GAME

Practice what you learn with the Mini Games.

Read the story about Maria's cat.

The clay cat is the main idea.

Details tell about the main idea.

Maria's Clay Cat

Maria made a clay cat.

Her cat has white eyes.

It has triangle ears.

It has a long, blue tail.

☑**Reading Check** Main Idea and Details

Underline the main idea.

Circle a detail about shape.

Senses

▶ VIDEO

Go online to watch
this video about
attentive listening.

Vocabulary

senses
structure
function

I can name the
five senses.

K-2-ETS1-1, K-2-ETS1-2

Jumpstart Discovery!

Think of a kitten. How
does its fur feel when you
touch it? Tell a partner.

How does it feel?

Science teachers help students to learn about things around them. They can teach about the way things feel. What sense can you use to tell how something feels?

Materials

- index cards
- objects (rock, stuffed animal, sandpaper, can)

Procedure

☐ 1. Think of words that tell how things feel.

☐ 2. Write each word.

☐ 3. Feel the objects.

☐ 4. Put a word next to each object.

Science Practice

You **carry out investigations** to learn more about objects.

Analyze and Interpret Data

5. **Identify** Which sense did you use?

_____

_____

The Five Senses

We have five senses.

Senses are ways our bodies tell us about the people and things around us.

They help us observe the world.

Senses help us learn.

Literacy ▸ Toolbox 🔍

Main Idea and Details Underline the main idea on this page.

Quest Connection

What senses can the students in Ms. Hall's class use to help them sort objects?

You touch with your skin.

Identify Circle the body parts that are used for each sense.

👆 **INTERACTIVITY**

Complete an activity about the senses.

You see with your eyes.

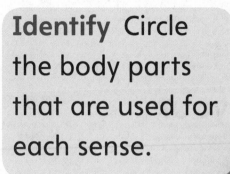

You hear with your ears.

You taste with your tongue.

You smell with your nose.

Structure and Function

Think about the objects in your classroom.

You can talk about the structure and function.

Structure is how an object is made or what is in it.

Function is what the object does, or how it works.

What can our senses tell us about structure and function?

Tools look different. They are made to do different jobs.

Use your senses. Match each tool to its function.

Describe Choose a tool. How would you use it at home?

Objects

Vocabulary
matter
change
shape

I can describe and sort objects.

K-2-ETS1-1

Jumpstart Discovery!

Play "I Spy."

Listen to clues about an object.

It is something you can see.

What is it?

How are objects the same?

Objects can be the same in some ways. How can you find out?

Materials
• various objects

Procedure

☐ **1.** Choose six objects.

☐ **2.** Ask your partner to sort them into two groups.

☐ **3.** Observe the two groups of objects.

Analyze and Interpret Data

4. Tell how the objects in each group are alike.

Science Practice

You **analyze data** from observations to compare objects.

Objects in Groups

Matter is anything that takes up space.

Objects are kinds of matter.

You can observe how they are the same.

round

Visual Literacy

Draw three objects in your classroom. Write a label for each object.

soft

INTERACTIVITY
Go online to learn more about sorting objects.

yellow

Quest Connection

Tell two ways you can sort objects.

Temperature and Weight

You sort objects in many ways.

Objects can be hot or cold.

Objects can be heavy or light.

Literacy ▸ Toolbox 🔧

Main Idea and Details What is the main idea? Draw a line under it.

Identify Circle heavy objects. Put an **X** on the hot objects.

You Can Change Matter

You can **change** objects.

You make them different.

You can **shape**, or make them into a different form.

You can cut or tear paper.

You can roll or cut clay.

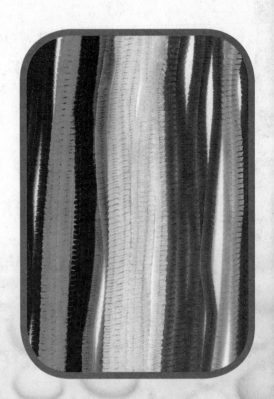

Identify Draw an **X** on the object you can bend. Circle the object you can melt.

How can you observe and sort objects?

How can you use your senses to help me clean up my classroom?

Suggested Materials

- box of objects
- closable sandwich bags for liquids
- tools for observing, such as a scale and hand lens

Procedure

☐ **1.** Choose one object.

☐ **2.** Draw or write your observations about the object. Identify a group for the object.

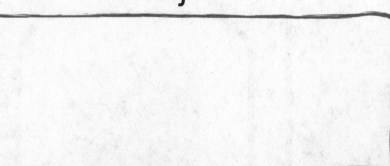

Science Practice

You can **analyze and interpret data** to sort objects into groups.

⚠ Do not taste any materials.

Analyze and Interpret Data

3. Tell a partner how you sorted the object.

Measure and Sort

You can sort long and short objects.

You can sort light and heavy objects.

Sort Work with a partner. Find five objects to measure. Measure your objects. Tell how you measured them.

scale

ruler

Solids, Liquids, and Gases

INTERACTIVITY

Go online to learn more about solids, liquids, and gases.

Vocabulary

solid
liquid
gas

I can observe the three states of matter.

K-2-ETS1-1

Jumpstart Discovery!

Pretend you are a balloon.

Act it out.

How do you feel?

What can you **observe** about **water?**

Why can you change the shape of water?

Procedure

☐ **1.** Observe the shape of the water.

☐ **2.** Think of ways to change its shape with the tools.

☐ **3.** Observe what the water does with each tool.

Analyze and Interpret Data

4. Which object can change its shape? Circle it.

cup   water   spoon

Materials

• water

• measuring cup

• small pitcher

• spoon

• funnel

Science Practice

You **make observations** to decide which tools are right for the job.

Solids, Liquids, and Gases

There are three kinds of matter.

A **solid** keeps its shape.

Tables and toys are solids.

A **liquid** can change its shape.

Water and milk are liquids.

A **gas** spreads out to fill its container.

The air around you is a gas.

Main Idea and Details
Underline the main idea.

Quest Connection

Tell a new way to sort objects.

Identify Three objects in the picture need labels. Write solid, liquid, or gas.

Engineering ▸ Toolbox

Asking Questions and Defining Problems
Look for matter in your classroom. What is a solid? How do you know? What questions can you ask to find out? See if you can find a liquid and a gas.

How will **you** sort solids, liquids, **and** gases?

Materials
- objects (solids, liquids, and gases)
- index cards

Use what you learned about matter to sort different types of matter.

Procedure

☐ **1.** Look at the objects.

☐ **2.** Make a plan to sort the objects by types of matter.

☐ **3.** Draw how you sorted the objects.

Science Practice

You **plan and conduct investigations** to learn about matter.

Analyze and Interpret Data

4. Observe your biggest group. Tell how you can make two smaller groups.

Observations

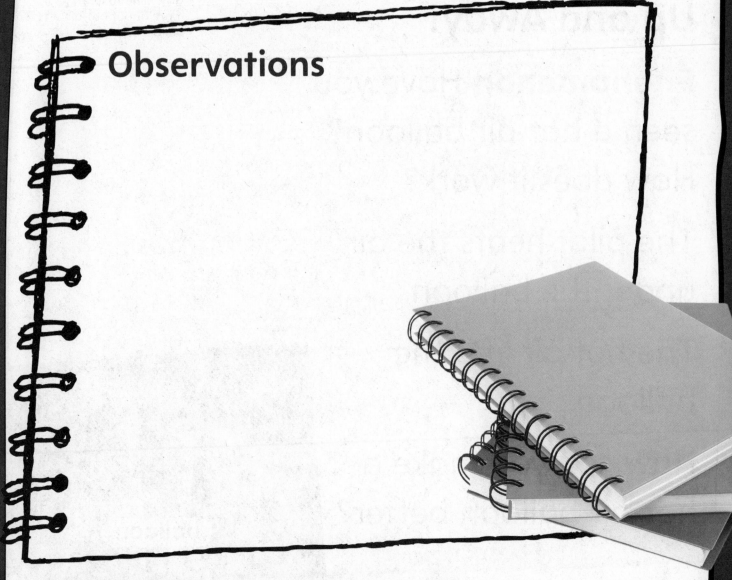

5. Imagine your groups of objects are centers in a science classroom. **Tell** a partner which center you will go to first. Why?

 INTERACTIVITY
Go online to learn more about hot-air balloons.

Up and Away!

Phenomenon Have you seen a hot-air balloon? How does it work?

The pilot heats the air under the balloon.

The hot air lifts the balloon.

How can you make a hot-air balloon better?

Improve It

☐ Look at the photo of the balloon.

☐ Find a way to make the balloon fly higher and farther.

balloon

wires

basket

62 Topic 2 Matter

- [ ] Draw a picture of your idea.
- [ ] Tell how your idea makes the balloon better.

☝ INTERACTIVITY

Go online to learn more about sorting objects for centers.

A Messy Classroom

How can we sort objects to put them away safely?

Show What You Found

Phenomenon Look at the objects in the classroom. Show the tools you can use to put them away.

Make It Better

Look at the tools you use to reach high shelves in your classroom. How can you make one of those tools better?

QUEST CHECK ✓ OFF

Science Teacher

Science teachers show students how to observe.

They teach students how to ask good questions.

They help students find the answers.

Science teachers love science!

Why do you think science teachers like their job?

_____

_____

_____

The Essential Question How can you classify different objects?

Show What You Learned
Tell a partner how to classify objects.

1. What is true about matter?
   a. It cannot be changed.
   b. It is how you see and hear.
   c. It takes up space.
   d. It is a way to test ideas.

2. Which one is a liquid?
   a. air
   b. brush
   c. pizza
   d. paint

3. What is the same about all the objects in the photos?

   a. same sound

   b. same color

   c. same size

   d. same shape

4. Mia wants to know how a rock feels. Which sense should she use?

   a. hear

   b. see

   c. smell

   d. touch

Read this scenario and answer questions 1–4.

Ella helped her mom.

They cleaned out the refrigerator.

Her mom got out the milk, water, and juice.

She put them on the top shelf.

She put meat and cheese in a drawer.

Ella sniffed an old bag of carrots.

"Yuck!" she said.

They didn't smell good.

She threw them out.

She put the other veggies in a bin.

1. What were Ella and her mom doing?

   a. getting ready to cook dinner

   b. throwing out food

   c. looking for something

   d. sorting objects

2. What sense did Ella use?

a. taste

b. smell

c. hearing

d. touch

3. Where did Ella's mom put liquids?

a. with the meat and cheese

b. on the top shelf

c. next to the veggie bin

d. under the solid food

4. Anything that takes up space is called ___.

a. size

b. solids

c. matter

d. change

How is one object different?

Phenomenon You use your senses to observe.

How can objects be different?

Procedure

☐ **1.** Choose three objects. Decide how two of the objects are the same.

☐ **2.** Have a partner observe the objects.

☐ **3.** Your partner tells why one object does not belong.

☐ **4.** Now let your partner have a turn.

☐ **5.** Draw or write your observations.

Materials
- small objects

Science Practice

You **ask questions** to find out how objects are used.

 Do not taste any materials.

Observations

How are some objects the same?	How is one different?

Analyze and Interpret Data

6. **Explain** Tell what senses you used.

Sunlight

Lesson 1 The Sun

Lesson 2 Sunlight and Earth's Surface

Next Generation Science Standards

K-PS3-1 Make observations to determine the effect of sunlight on Earth's surface.

K-PS3-2 Use tools and materials to design and build a structure that will reduce the warming effect of sunlight on an area.

Go online to access your digital course.

- VIDEO
- eTEXT
- INTERACTIVITY
- SCIENCE SONG
- GAME
- ASSESSMENT

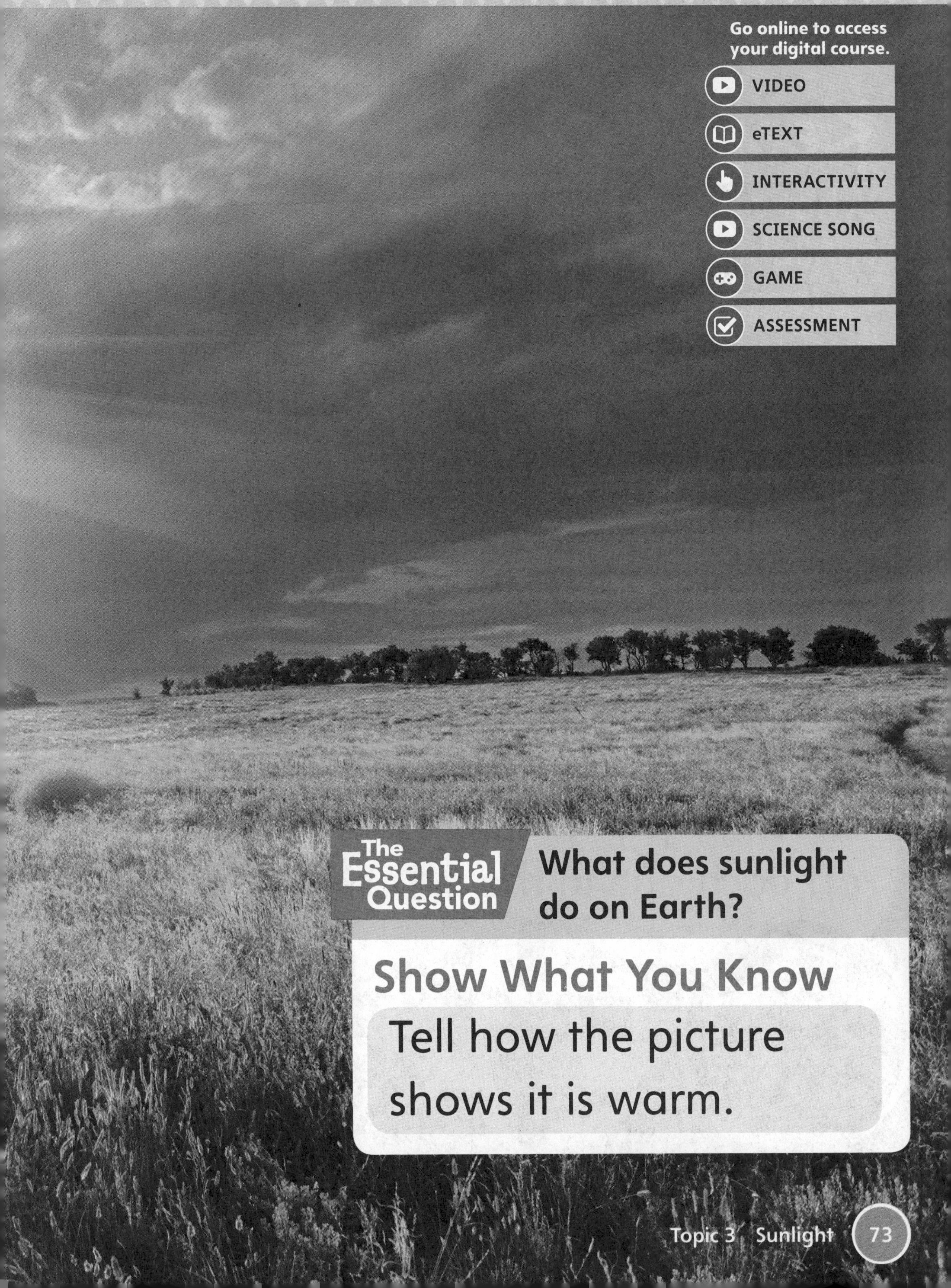

The Essential Question What does sunlight do on Earth?

Show What You Know

Tell how the picture shows it is warm.

Keep It Cool

What can you design to keep sunlight off of a dog?

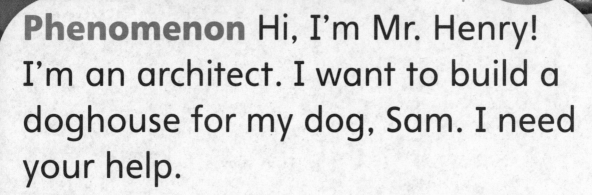

Phenomenon Hi, I'm Mr. Henry! I'm an architect. I want to build a doghouse for my dog, Sam. I need your help.

How can I keep Sam cool on sunny days? Help me plan and design the doghouse. Look for ideas as you read. Follow the path. Do each lesson to plan a doghouse. Check off each one in the QUEST CHECK ✓ OFF .

Next Generation Science Standards

K-PS3-1 Make observations to determine the effect of sunlight on Earth's surface.

K-PS3-2 Use tools and materials to design and build a structure that will reduce the warming effect of sunlight on an area.

Quest Check-In 1

Lesson 1

Use what you learned about the sun to tell how to protect the dog.

Quest Check-In Lab 2

Lesson 2

You learned how the sun warms Earth. Test how different materials reduce the effects of sunlight.

Quest Findings

Finish your Quest. Find a fun way to show and tell about your doghouse.

What can you observe about the sun?

Scientists observe by using their senses. How does sunlight feel on your body?

Procedure

☐ **1.** Find ways to test how sunlight feels.

☐ **2.** Tell your teacher about your ideas before you start.

☐ **3.** Fill in the chart.

Analyze and Interpret Data

4. Explain where you felt warmer. Tell why.

Materials

- Sunlight Chart

Science Practice

You make observations when you use your senses.

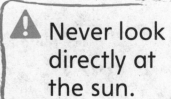 Never look directly at the sun.

Picture Clues

Scientists ask questions and look for answers. Sometimes they get clues from pictures.

GAME
Practice what you learn with the Mini Games.

Stay Cool

The sun keeps animals warm. It can make some animals too warm.

☑ **Reading Check** **Picture Clues**

Look at the pictures. Write the missing word in the sentences.

1. The goats are trying

   to stay _____

   under the tree.

2. The snake warms itself by

   staying in the _____ .

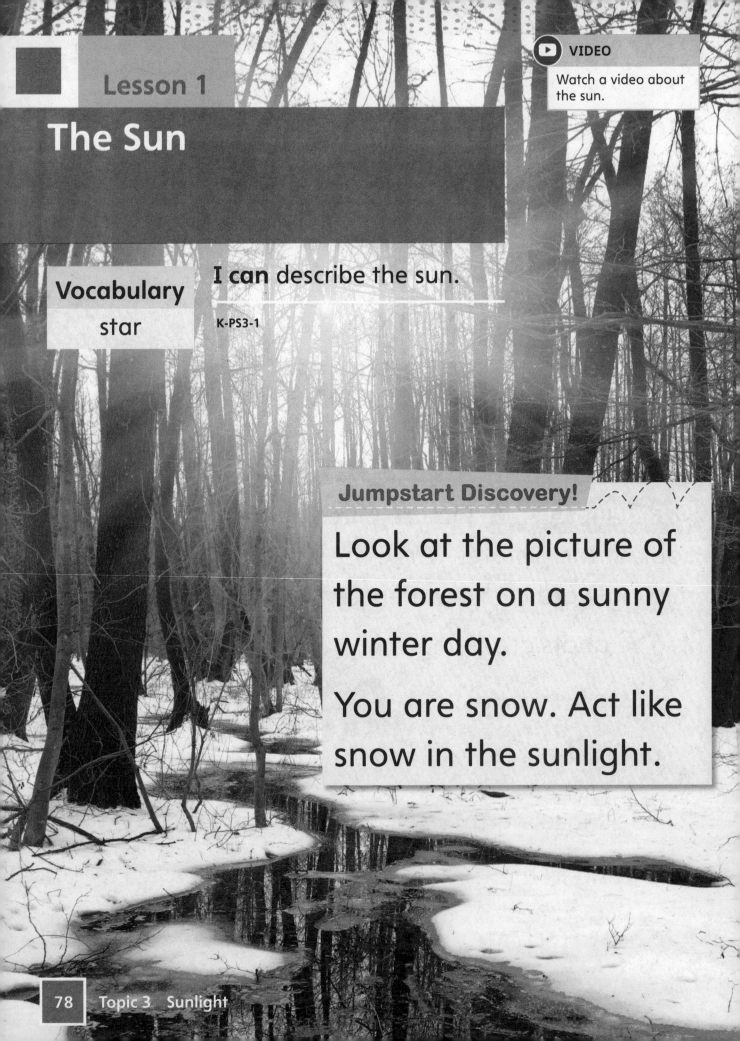

The Sun

▶ VIDEO
Watch a video about the sun.

Vocabulary

star

I can describe the sun.

K-PS3-1

Jumpstart Discovery!

Look at the picture of the forest on a sunny winter day.

You are snow. Act like snow in the sunlight.

What can the (sun) do?

Scientists analyze and interpret data to answer their questions. How can you use the data from this lab to answer the question, "What can the sun do?"

Materials
- ice cubes
- 2 containers

Science Practice

Compare data you collected in a chart.

Procedure

☐ **1.** Use the materials to show what the sun can do.

☐ **2.** Record your data in the chart.

Container	Sun	Shade	What happened?

Analyze and Interpret Data

3. Explain how you used observations to learn about the sun.

The Sun and Earth

A **star** is a big, hot ball of gas.

The sun is a star.

The sun gives Earth light.

The sun gives Earth heat.

Literacy ▸ Toolbox 🔍

Picture Clues Look at the picture.

What kind of day do you see? Tell how you know.

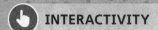
The sun is the largest object in the daytime sky.

The sun is very big, but it looks small from Earth.

That is because the sun is so far away.

Ask a Question What would you like to know about the sun? Write a question.

_____

_____

_____

_____

Quest Connection

▼▼▼▼▼▼▼▼▼▼▼▼▼▼▼▼▼▼▼▼▼

Tell two ways a doghouse can protect Mr. Henry's dog.

Staying Cool

Look at the parts of a
doghouse.

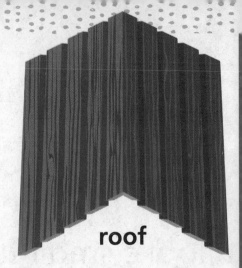

roof

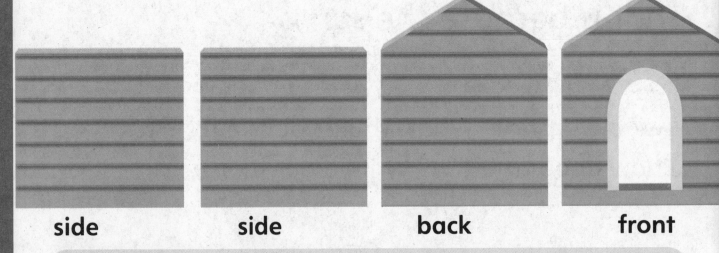

side   side   back   front

Draw Draw a plan for your dog house.

Copy the labels on to each part.

Explain all of the parts.

Storms on the Sun

The sun has storms! These storms can cause many problems on Earth. Your computer might not work. The internet might not work!

Scientists are working now to try to solve these problems. They try to predict when these storms might reach Earth. Scientists want everyone to be prepared.

solar storm

Describe What does a solar storm look like?

uEngineer It! Model STEM

INTERACTIVITY

Go online to learn more about how engineers solve problems.

Sunny Days

Phenomenon It is a very warm, sunny day outside. You are very hot! You need to make something to keep sunlight off your head and face.

Model It

Look around you. Observe what makes shade. Think about the following questions. Answer them as you make your model.

☐ How can you make something to keep sunlight off your head?

☐ What will you use to block sunlight?

☐ What materials will you need?

1. Draw a plan.

2. Explain your model.
Tell how it will work in sunshine.

Sunlight and Earth's Surface

Vocabulary
Earth

I can observe how sunlight warms everything on Earth's surface.

K-PS3-1, K-PS3-2

Jumpstart Discovery!

Choose an animal. Act out what the animal does in the sun. Act out what the animal does in the shade.

Which objects change in the sun?

What happens when sunlight shines on objects on Earth's surface? How can you find out?

Procedure

☐ **1.** Choose 3 objects to test.

☐ **2.** Make a plan to test them.

☐ **3.** Show your plan to your teacher.

☐ **4.** Observe what happens.

☐ **5.** Fill in the Objects in the Sun chart.

Analyze and Interpret Data

6. Explain Tell how the objects that changed are alike.

Materials

• Objects in the Sun chart

Suggested Materials

• crayon
• clay
• ice cube
• black fabric
• white fabric
• metal object
• wood object
• dark-colored trays
• rocks
• sand
• soil

Science Practice

You **collect data** when you make observations.

The Sun Warms Earth

The sun helps us stay alive.

It warms everything on Earth.

Earth is the planet where we live.

 VIDEO

Watch a video about sunlight and Earth's surface.

☑ Reading Check **Picture Clues**

Write a caption for the picture. Tell about how the sun warms Earth.

_____

_____

_____

_____

The sun warms the land.

The sun warms the water.

The sun warms the air.

Land cools when it is not in sunlight.

Water cools when it is not in sunlight.

Air cools when it is not in sunlight.

Engineering Practice ▸ Toolbox 🔧

Design a Solution
Stand by a window. Think of ways to block sunlight. Tell your ideas to a partner.

Identify Fill in the chart. List two things the sun warms in each place.

What Sunlight Warms on Earth		
On Land	**In Water**	**In Air**

Sunlight and Earth

Sunlight causes many changes on Earth.

👆 **INTERACTIVITY**

Learn how the sun changes the temperature on Earth.

☑ **Reading Check** **Picture Clues**

What happens to water, rocks, and sand in sunlight?

_____

_____

_____

_____

Sunlight warms water.

Sunlight warms sand.

Sunlight warms rocks.

Quest Connection

Tell how sunlight warms everything on Earth.

Sunlight warms soil.

STEM Quest Check-In Lab

Which material makes the best roof?

Which materials reduce the warming effect of sunlight?

Suggested Materials
- thermometers
- sheets of clear plastic wrap
- sheets of aluminum foil
- sandpaper
- pieces of plywood
- squares of canvas

Test Your Design

☐ 1. Make a plan to test which materials reduce the warming effect of sunlight. Use the thermometer. Choose three materials to build three model roofs.

☐ 2. Show your plan to your teacher.

☐ 3. Test your materials.

Engineering Practice
Engineers use tools to solve a problem.

92 Topic 3 Sunlight

Observations

Material	Time in the Sun	Temperature

Evaluate Your Design

4. Tell which materials kept the thermometer cooler?

5. Tell which materials made the thermometer heat up?

6. **Explain** Tell what you learned to a partner.

INTERACTIVITY

Apply what you learned in the Quest.

Keep It Cool

What can you design to keep sunlight off of a dog?

Phenomenon What materials and design will you use for Sam's doghouse?

It should keep Sam cool when it is hot and sunny outside.

Show What You Found

Gather your materials and build a doghouse. Then look at other doghouses. How can you improve your design?

QUEST CHECK ✓ OFF

Architect

Architects plan buildings.

They draw rooms, walls, and a roof for their buildings.

They choose materials to use.

What if all the walls in your home were made of glass?

Tell if this is a good idea. Why or why not?

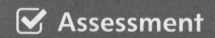

The Essential Question   **What does sunlight do on Earth?**

Show What You Learned

Tell a partner what you learned about how the sun warms Earth.

1. What is the sun?

   a. a moon in the night sky

   b. a planet in the sky

   c. an object that is close to Earth

   d. a star in the sky

2. What do we get from the sun?

   a. heat and light

   b. food and water

   c. hot and cold rays

   d. rocks and soil

3. What is one effect that sunlight has on Earth?

a. Sunlight brings snow.

b. Sunlight warms the land.

c. Sunlight brings cold air.

d. Sunlight helps new rocks grow.

4. Why does the sun look small in the sky?

a. The sun is closer to Earth than the moon.

b. The moon and the sun are the same size.

c. The sun is far away.

d. The sun is smaller than Earth.

Read and answer questions 1–3.

Zac works at an animal shelter.

The dogs have an outdoor play area.

But it gets very hot in the sun.

How can Zac keep the dogs cool on a bright, sunny day?

Zac drew two ideas to help.

1. Which idea will work better? Circle the letter.

a.    b.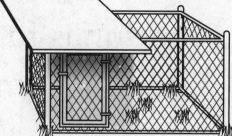

2. What is Zac trying to do?

    a. stop the dogs from running away

    b. keep the dogs in a safe place

    c. give the dogs a shady place

    d. build a climbing place for the dogs

3. Which part of this kennel will be coolest on a sunny day? Circle the letter.

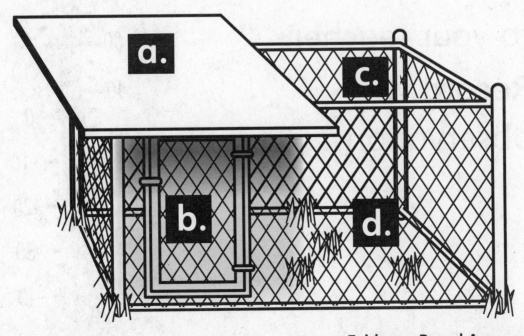

Where is it warmer?

Materials
• 2 thermometers

Phenomenon A scientist uses tools to make observations.

How can you use a thermometer to make observations?

Science Practice

You can use **tools** to help you make observations.

Procedure

☐ **1.** Use the thermometers to observe the effects of sunlight.

☐ **2.** Make a plan. Show it to your teacher.

☐ **3.** **Record** your observations.

Observations

Warmer or Cooler?			
Thermometer 1	Starting	In the Shade	Warmer or Cooler?
Thermometer 2	Starting	In the Sun	Warmer or Cooler?

Analyze and Interpret Data

4. **Communicate** What do you observe about sunlight?

_____

_____

_____

5. **Evidence** How can you support your observations?

_____

_____

_____

Earth's Weather

Next Generation Science Standards

K-ESS2-1 Use and share observations of local weather conditions to describe patterns over time. **K-ESS3-2** Ask questions to obtain information about the purpose of weather forecasting to prepare for, and respond to, severe weather. **K-2-ETS1-1** Ask questions, make observations, and gather information about a situation people want to change to define a simple problem that can be solved through the development of a new or improved object or tool. **K-2-ETS1-2** Develop a simple sketch, drawing, or physical model to illustrate how the shape of an object helps it function as needed to solve a given problem. **K-2-ETS1-3** Analyze data from tests of two objects designed to solve the same problem to compare the strengths and weaknesses of how each performs.

The Essential Question How does the weather change?

Show What You Know

What is your favorite weather?
Do you know what causes it?
Tell a partner what you know.

Chasing Storms

How does weather change when a storm is coming?

Phenomenon Hi! My name is Ms. Lopez. I am a storm chaser. I follow and study storms. Our town is planning a summer festival. We want to make sure people stay safe if there is a storm. Help me make a safety poster. The poster needs to tell people how to stay safe in storms. Follow the path. Do each activity with a  .

Quest Check-In 1

Lesson 1

Use what you learned about types of weather.

Next Generation Science Standards

K-ESS2-1 Use and share observations of local weather conditions to describe patterns over time.

K-ESS3-2 Ask questions to obtain information about the purpose of weather forecasting to prepare for, and respond to, severe weather.

VIDEO

Watch a video about a storm chaser.

Quest Check-In 3

Lesson 3 ◆

Learn more about weather and storms in different seasons.

Quest Check-In Lab 4

Lesson 4 ▲

Make a tool that measures wind. Describe how wind changes. Tell how people use wind to study storms.

Quest Check-In 2

Lesson 2 ●

Observe the weather. Predict weather patterns where you live.

Quest Findings

Complete the Quest! Make a safety poster that tells people how to stay safe in a storm.

How does the weather change during the day?

How can you use weather information to plan your day?

Materials
- School Day Forecast Sheet

Procedure

☐ 1. Look at the School Day Forecast Sheet. Tell how the temperature changes.

☐ 2. Observe the temperature and weather. Record your data.

Science Practice

You **get information** to help answer a scientific question.

Analyze and Interpret Data

3. **Evidence** Tell how the temperature changes during the day.

4. **Ask Questions** Ask a question about weather patterns.

Main Idea and Details

The main idea is what the sentences are about. Details tell about the main idea.

 GAME

Practice what you learn with the Mini Games.

A Stormy Day

There was a big storm. The clouds were dark and gray. The wind blew hard. It rained a lot. There were puddles everywhere. What a storm!

☑ **Reading Check** **Main Idea and Details** Circle the main idea. Underline at least two details.

Different Kinds of Weather

▶ **VIDEO**

Watch a video about different kinds of weather.

Vocabulary

snow

temperature

I can describe different types of weather.

K-ESS2-1, K-ESS3-2

Jumpstart Discovery!

What is the weather like today? Tell a partner two words that describe today's weather.

How can you make it rain?

Many storms have rain. How can you make a model of rain?

Procedure

☐ 1. Fill the jar about 2/3 full with water.

☐ 2. Put shaving cream on top of the water.

☐ 3. Put several drops of colored water on the shaving cream.

☐ 4. Tell a partner what you observe.

Analyze and Interpret Data

5. **Explain** Why do you think it rained in the jar? Tell a partner.

Materials

- jar
- tap water
- shaving cream
- colored water
- eye dropper or pipette

Science Practice

You **develop and use models** to explain phenomena.

Temperature

Temperature tells us how hot or cold it is outside.

When it is hot outside, you can play in the water.

When it is cold outside, you wear a jacket and a hat.

Identify Underline something you can wear when it is cold.

hot

snow

cold

Sunny and Not Sunny

Some days the sun shines bright.

It is sunny.

Sometimes, it is cloudy. We do not see the sun.

On other days, it rains. If it is cold enough, it will snow.

Snow is frozen water that falls from the sky.

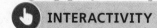
INTERACTIVITY
Go online to learn more about how weather can change.

sunny day

cloudy day

Quest Connection

What can Ms. Lopez tell people about when it might snow?

rainy day

Wind

Wind is moving air.

There is a lot of wind on some days.

There is only a little wind on other days.

It can be windy on a sunny day.

It can be windy on a rainy day.

It can be windy on a snowy day.

Weather Words

The pictures show different kinds of weather.

Match the weather words to the correct pictures.

Sunny   Cloudy   Rainy

uEngineer It! Build STEM

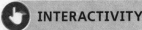

INTERACTIVITY

Go online to learn more about how to solve design problems.

Don't Blow Away!

Phenomenon Some people use a tent at parks or the beach. It keeps the sun off them. The tent can blow over in the wind. It can even blow away!

Can you build a tent that will not blow away?

Build It

☐ Decide which materials to use.

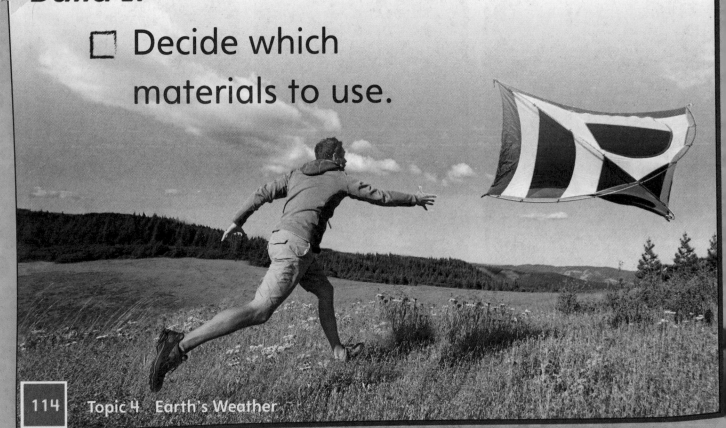

☐ Decide what each material will do. Use the table to help you plan.

☐ Build your tent.

☐ Test your tent using a fan.

Observations

Material	What it will do

What happened when you tested your tent?

_____

- - - - - - - - - - - - - - - - -

_____

Tell a partner how you can make your tent better.

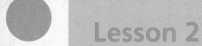

Lesson 2

Weather Patterns

▶ VIDEO

Go online to learn more about weather patterns.

Vocabulary

pattern

I can observe that weather changes from day to day.

I can observe patterns in the weather.

K-ESS2-1, K-2-ETS1-2

Jumpstart Discovery!

Act out some things you can do when it rains.

HANDS-ON LAB

K-ESS2-1, K-2-ETS1-2, SEP.3, SEP.4

How can you collect rain?

How can you measure how much rain fell?

Procedure

Materials

- 2-liter plastic bottles
- pebbles
- water
- Rain Collection Sheet

☐ **1.** Use the materials.

☐ **2.** Make a rain collector. Make measurement markers.

☐ **3.** Put your rain collector outside. Record your data on the Rain Collection Sheet.

Science Practice

You can **design a solution** to answer a question or solve a problem.

Analyze and Interpret Data

4. Record Answer the questions on the Rain Collection Sheet.

Sun or Rain

Weather happens in patterns.

A **pattern** is something that happens over and over.

Weather follows patterns during a year.

There are often many sunny days in summer.

There are often many cloudy and rainy days during fall.

The same patterns happen each year.

Hot or Cold Weather

It is usually hot for a few months in the year.

It is colder other months.

Some months it is not too hot or too cold.

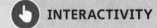

INTERACTIVITY

Go online to learn more about recording the weather.

Quest Connection

Tell how Ms. Lopez uses patterns to predict temperature.

Weather in Different Places

Different places have different weather.

These are patterns.

Some places have hot weather all year.

Some places have more rain than other places.

Some places have snow for most of the year.

Visual Literacy Tell how the weather patterns are different in these two places.

Quest Check-In

Predict the Weather

1. Complete the table.
   What will the weather be in different months?

   Where I live

   _____

   _____

	Example	Now	in 1 month	in 2 months
Month	January			
Temperature	Cold			
Types of Weather	Snow, ice			
Things People Do	Sled			

2. What do you think the weather will be like in four months?

   _____

   _____

Seasons

 VIDEO
Watch a video about seasons.

Vocabulary
season

I can describe the seasons.

K-ESS2-1

Jumpstart Discovery!

Think about your favorite season. Tell a partner some things you like to do during that season.

What is the (weather) like in different seasons?

How does the weather change in different seasons?

Materials
• 4 index cards

Procedure

☐ **1.** Draw a picture of a season on a card.

☐ **2.** Write words about that season on the back of the card.

☐ **3.** Make a card for each season.

Analyze and Interpret Data

4. Compare your cards.
Tell how your cards are the same and different.

_____

_____

_____

Different Seasons

Many parts of the world have four **seasons**.

Each season has different weather.

Math ▸ Toolbox

Measure You can use many different tools to measure snowfall. Name some tools you might use.

It is cold in the winter.

There are no leaves on trees.

☑ **Reading Check** | **Main Idea and Details** Circle a detail about something that happens in spring.

In the fall, it gets cooler.

Leaves fall off the trees.

INTERACTIVITY

Go online to learn more about how weather changes with the seasons.

It gets warmer in the spring.

Plants start to grow.

Quest Connection

Choose a photo. Tell how Ms. Lopez might describe weather in that photo.

In the summer, it is hot.

Plants keep growing.

Seasonal Changes

Choose a season.

Draw a scene of that season.

Draw leaves on the tree to match the season.

Label the season.

Explain Tell a partner about the weather in that season.

Thundersnow

Boom! What was that? Thunder during a snow storm?

Sometimes you hear thunder and see lightning when it rains.

Sometimes, there is thunder and lightning when it is snowing.

It is cold outside.

This is called thundersnow.

Explain Tell how thundersnow is different different from a regular thunderstorm?

Severe Weather

▶ VIDEO

Watch a video about storms.

Vocabulary

thunderstorm
tornado
hurricane

I can understand why it is important to prepare for severe weather.

K-ESS2-1, K-ESS3-2, K-2-ETS1-2

Jumpstart Discovery!

Some scientists tell us when big storms are coming. What questions can you ask the scientists about what they do?

What does a (storm) look like?

How can you make a model of a storm?

Materials

- jar with lid
- dish soap
- water
- vinegar
- glitter

Procedure

☐ 1. Put all the materials in the jar.

☐ 2. Swirl the jar. Observe what happens. Draw what you see on a sheet of paper.

Science Practice

You **use models** to find out how something happens in real life.

Analyze and Interpret Data

3. **Explain** What happened to the glitter when you swirled the jar?

_____

- - - - - - - - - - - - - - - - -

Thunderstorms and Tornadoes

A **thunderstorm** is a storm with lightning, thunder, and rain.

Some thunderstorms make tornadoes.

A **tornado** is a type of storm. Most tornadoes happen in the middle of the United States.

tornado

A tornado has very fast winds that turn in a circle.

The winds can pick things up and move them.

thunderstorm

Explain How can a tornado pick up things?

_____

- - - - - - - - - - - - - - - -

_____

_____

- - - - - - - - - - - - - - - -

_____

Hurricanes

Hurricanes are big storms that form over warm water in the ocean.

They happen on the east coast. They happen in places such as the Gulf of Mexico.

They can move onto land that is near the ocean.

Hurricanes have strong winds and a lot of rain.

They can last for many days.

hurricane

Crosscutting Concepts ▸ Toolbox

Systems A hurricane is a system. The middle is the eye. It is the calmest part. The eyewall is next to the eye. It has the highest winds. It does the most damage on land. Share with a partner other storms that are like hurricanes.

Quest Connection

Tell why Ms. Lopez might want to warn people about hurricanes.

Be Prepared

Storms can be dangerous.

The power can stop working. Trees can fall.

People should have flashlights and batteries.

They need to find shelter during a storm.

👆 INTERACTIVITY

Go online to learn more about tools scientists use to predict weather.

☑ **Reading Check** **Main Idea and Details** Circle a reason why it is important to get ready for storms.

Weather Forecasts

Weather scientists look for patterns in local weather.

They can make a forecast.

Weather scientists can warn people about severe weather.

People can respond to severe weather.

How does the wind *move?*

Materials
- pinwheel
- electric fan

Storm chasers measure weather. How can you measure the wind?

Science Practice

You **develop and use models** to study phenomena.

⚠ Do not stick anything in the fan.

Procedure

☐ **1.** Use the materials. Collect data on wind.

☐ **2.** Make a plan. Show your teacher.

☐ **3.** Put your observations in the table.

Fan speed	What happened
Low	
High	

Analyze and Interpret Data

4. **Describe** What happened when the speed of the fan changed?

_____

- - - - - - - - - - - - - - - - -

_____

5. **Ask Questions** Write a question about using the pinwheel.

_____

- - - - - - - - - - - - - - - - -

_____

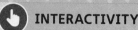 **INTERACTIVITY**

Go online to learn more about severe weather.

Chasing Storms

How does weather change when a storm is coming?

Phenomenon Your town is planning an outdoor festival. There may be severe weather. Make a safety poster. Include questions people have about severe weather. Show what people can do to stay safe.

Show What You Found

Tell a partner something we should put on a safety poster to warn people about storms.

Storm Chaser

Storm chasers study all kinds of storms. Some storm chasers also talk about weather on TV. Storm chasers take pictures of storms.

Some storm chasers fly into hurricanes on airplanes.

What kind of storm would you study if you were a storm chaser?

_____

- -

_____

_____

The Essential Question

How does the weather change?

Tell a partner what you learned about how the weather can change.

1. Which word describes something that happens over and over?

   a. Pattern

   b. Weather

   c. Season

   d. Chart

2. What may fall when the weather is so cold that water freezes?

   a. Rain

   b. Wind

   c. Snow

   d. Leaves

3. In which season do leaves fall off trees?

   a. winter

   b. spring

   c. fall

   d. summer

4. Look at the weather report. Then, fill in the chart.

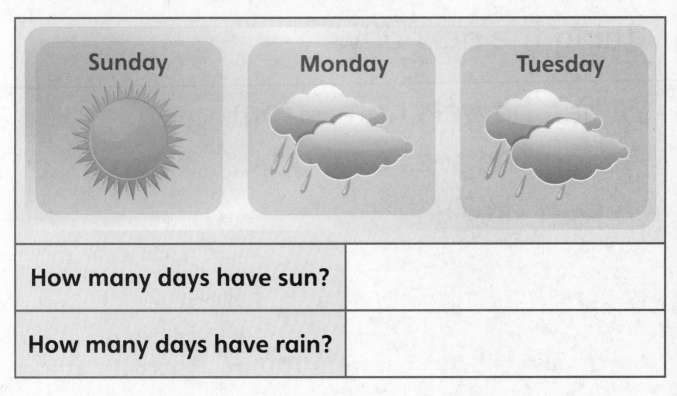

Sunday	Monday	Tuesday

How many days have sun?	
How many days have rain?	

Read this scenario and answer the questions.

Akiko wakes up in the morning and gets ready for school. He needs to wear a jacket. During recess, he does not need a jacket. He notices the same thing the next day.

When he gets home from school, he sees a weather report on TV.

Friday	Saturday	Sunday

33°C (91°F)	33°C (91°F)	25°C (77°F)

1. How did the weather change between morning and recess?

_____

- - - - - - - - - - - - - - - - -

_____

2. How many days in the weather report show hot weather?

a. 0   **b.** 1

c. 2   **d.** 3

3. Name something Akiko might wear outside on Sunday.

_____

- - - - - - - - - - - - - - - - -

_____

4. How will the weather change from Friday to Saturday?

a. It will get hot.

b. There will be rain.

c. It will get cloudy.

d. There will be a storm.

What is the **weather** like?

Phenomenon Scientists record what the weather is like each day. This helps them learn how the weather can change. You can do this, too.

Procedure

☐ 1. **Observe** the weather each day.

☐ 2. Record your observations on the Weather Data Sheet. You can use weather words or draw pictures.

Materials

- Weather Data Sheet
- crayons

Science Practice

You **observe** to identify patterns.

Analyze and Interpret Data

3. What pattern do you notice in your observations?

_____

- -

_____

4. **Compare** your observations with those of a partner. What do you notice?

_____

- -

_____

5. How would your observations be different if you observed the weather in another season?

_____

- -

Needs of Living Things

Next Generation Science Standard

K-LS1-1 Use observations to describe patterns of what plants and animals (including humans) need to survive. **K-2-ETS1-1** Ask questions, make observations, and gather information about a situation people want to change or define a simple problem that can be solved though the development of a new or improved object or tool. **K-2-ETS1-2** Develop a simple sketch, drawing, or physical model to illustrate how the shape of an object helps it function as needed to solve a given problem.

The Essential Question What do plants and animals need to survive?

Show What You Know

Draw a circle on things plants and animals need to live.

145

Let's Build a Park

What do plants and animals need to live in a park?

Phenomenon Hi! My name is Ms. Chen. I am a wildlife biologist. The town is building a new park. Help me make a book that shows the things plants and animals will need to live in the park. The path shows the Quest activities you will complete as you work through the topic. Check off your progress each time you complete an activity with a QUEST CHECK ✓ OFF .

Lesson 1 ■
Show what plants need to live in the park.

Next Generation Science Standard
K-LS1-1 Use observations to describe patterns of what plants and animals (including humans) need to survive.

Quest Check-In 3

Lesson 3 ◆

Tell what people will need to be able to spend a day in the park.

 VIDEO

Watch a video about a wildlife biologist.

Quest Check-In Lab 4

Lesson 4 ▲

Learn what caterpillars need to live so that the park can have beautiful butterflies.

Quest Check-In 2

Lesson 2 ●

Identify what the fish in a koi pond need to live.

Quest Findings

Complete the Quest! Draw a picture of what the park should look like so that plants and animals can live there.

What if plants do not get what they need?

What observations can you make to answer the question in the title?

Procedure

☐ 1. **Observe** the photos of the plants.

☐ 2. Record your observations.

Analyze and Interpret Data

3. **Evaluate** Which plant is getting what it needs? Tell a partner.

Alike and Different

Wildlife biologists observe animals. Read about ways big cats and pet cats are alike and different.

🎮 **GAME**

Practice what you learn with the Mini Games.

Big Cats and Pet Cats

Big cats and pet cats both need food and water to live. Big cats, like tigers, must find their own food and water. Pet cats get food and water from their owners.

pet cat

✓ **Reading Check**   **Alike and Different**

Circle a way tigers and pet cats are alike. Underline a way they are different.

tiger

Needs of Plants

VIDEO

Go online to watch a video about how plants use air, water, and sunlight to grow.

Vocabulary
survive
pattern

I can tell what plants need to survive.

K-LS1-1

Jumpstart Discovery!

How does a sunflower plant get what it needs? Act it out.

How do plants get water?

Wildlife biologists observe plants. How can you observe a plant getting water?

Procedure

☐ 1. Make a plan to show how water moves through a plant.

☐ 2. Predict what will happen when you put the plant in water.

☐ 3. **Observe** the flower. Record your observations on the Colored Flower Sheet.

Analyze and Interpret Data

4. **Use Data** Tell how water moves in a plant.

Materials

- white carnations
- water
- food coloring
- clear container
- Colored Flower Sheet
- crayons

Science Practice

You **analyze data** when you record observations.

Plants Need Sunlight

Survive means to live.

Plants need sunlight to live and grow.

Sunlight helps plants make food.

Plants do not need to get food from somewhere else.

Crosscutting Concepts ▶ Toolbox

Patterns A **pattern** is something that is the same over and over again. What pattern do you notice about what plants need?

Plants Need Air

Plants need air to survive.

Gases in the air help plants make their food.

Identify Circle two things on these pages that plants need.

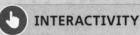

INTERACTIVITY

Go online to learn more about what plants need.

Plants Need Water

Plants need water.

Water helps plants make their food.

Water can come from rain.

Water can also come from people.

Literacy ▸ Toolbox 🔧

Alike and Different
Circle a sentence about how plants are alike.

Quest Connection

Tell a partner two things that Ms. Chen should put in the book.

Caring for Plants at the Park

Look at things that could go in the park.

Identify Circle the things plants will need to survive.

Evaluate Put an **X** on the things plants do not need to survive.

Needs of Animals

▶ VIDEO

Go online to learn more about the types of food animals eat.

Vocabulary
gills

I can tell what animals need to survive.

K-LS1-1, K-2-ETS1-2

Jumpstart Discovery!

Think about a bear. What will a bear need to live? Tell a partner.

Which (feet) do the best job?

Animals need their feet to move and to get food. How can you build a model of an animal's feet?

Procedure

☐ 1. Use the images to see how an animal's feet help them.

☐ 2. Make a plan to build a model of an animal's feet.

☐ 3. Build your model.

Analyze and Interpret Data

4. **Explain** How does your model animal use its feet where it lives? Tell a partner.

_____

. . . .

Materials

- felt
- construction paper
- cardboard
- tape
- glue
- crayons
- scissors
- pipe cleaners

Science Practice

You **use models** to learn how things work.

⚠ Be careful with scissors!

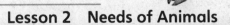

Animals Need Food

Animals must eat food.

Some animals eat plants.
Some animals eat other
animals.

Animals live where they can
get the food they need.

Identify Put an **X** on a picture
of something an animal eats.

Math ▸ Toolbox

Count How
many of these
animals eat
plants? How
many animals
eat animals?

Animals Need Water

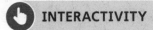
INTERACTIVITY

Go online to learn more about things animals need.

All living things need water to survive.

Animals can get water from many different places.

Animals can get water from rain, rivers, and ponds.

People give animals water, too.

Quest Connection

What should Ms. Chen put in the book for animals? Tell how you know.

Animals Need Air

Animals need air to survive.

Some animals get air through their noses and mouths. A wolf uses its nose and mouth to get air.

Fish get air through their gills.

Gills take air out of the water for fish.

☑ **Reading Check** **Alike and Different** Circle words that tell how fish and wolves are different.

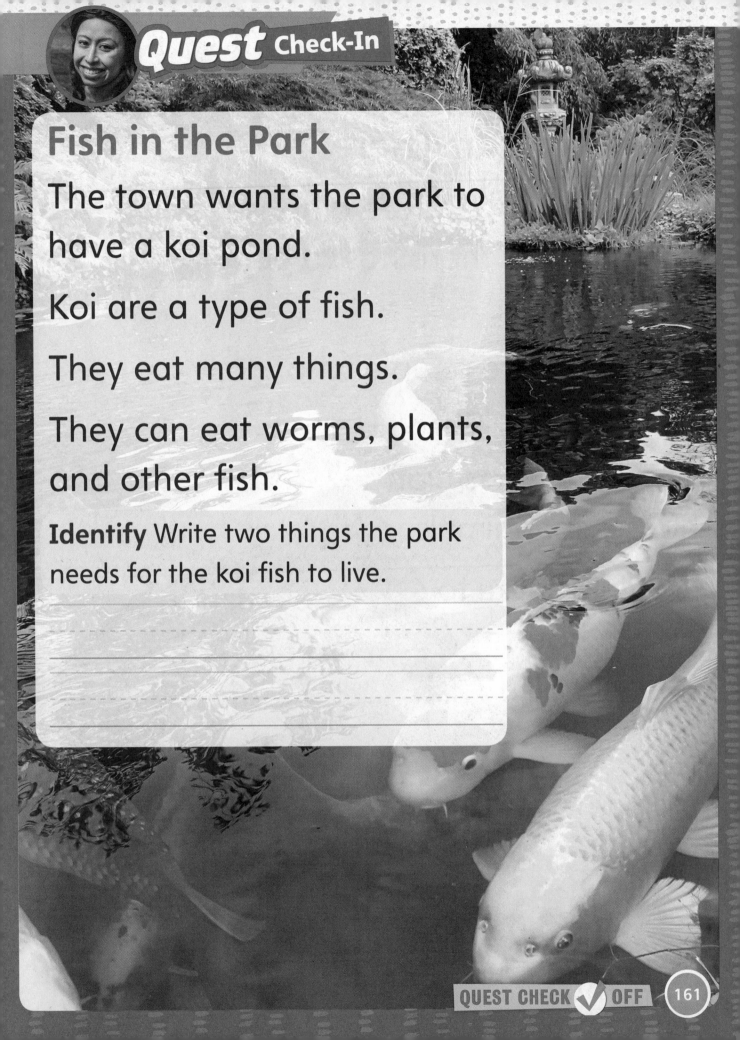

Fish in the Park

The town wants the park to have a koi pond.

Koi are a type of fish.

They eat many things.

They can eat worms, plants, and other fish.

Identify Write two things the park needs for the koi fish to live.

_____

_____

_____

K-2-ETS1-1, K-2-ETS1-2, SEP.1, SEP.6

 INTERACTIVITY

Go online to learn more about building animal shelters.

It Is Cold Out There!

Phenomenon Before a house can be built, there has to be a plan.

Architects are people who draw these plans.

Some architects plan houses for animals.

Would you like to plan a house for animals?

Design It

Birds can get cold in the winter. Plan a house that will help keep the birds warm.

- ☐ Decide what materials to use on the outside and the inside.

- ☐ Draw what the house should look like.

Lesson 3
Needs of People

VIDEO

Go online to watch a video about things that people need to live.

Vocabulary
shelter

I can tell what people need to survive.

K-LS1-1

Jumpstart Discovery!

How do you feel when you haven't eaten in a long time? Act it out.

What should you wear?

Clothing is something people need. How do you decide what clothes to wear?

Procedure

☐ **1.** Color the clothing items. Cut them out.

☐ **2.** Add them to the season you would use them.

Analyze and Interpret Data

3. Identify How did the clothing you used change? Tell a partner.

4. Draw Conclusions Describe one way clothing gives you something you need.

_____

_____

_____

Materials

- Clothing and Weather Sheet
- crayons
- safety scissors

Science Practice

You **analyze data** to find patterns.

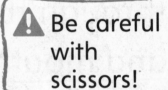 Be careful with scissors!

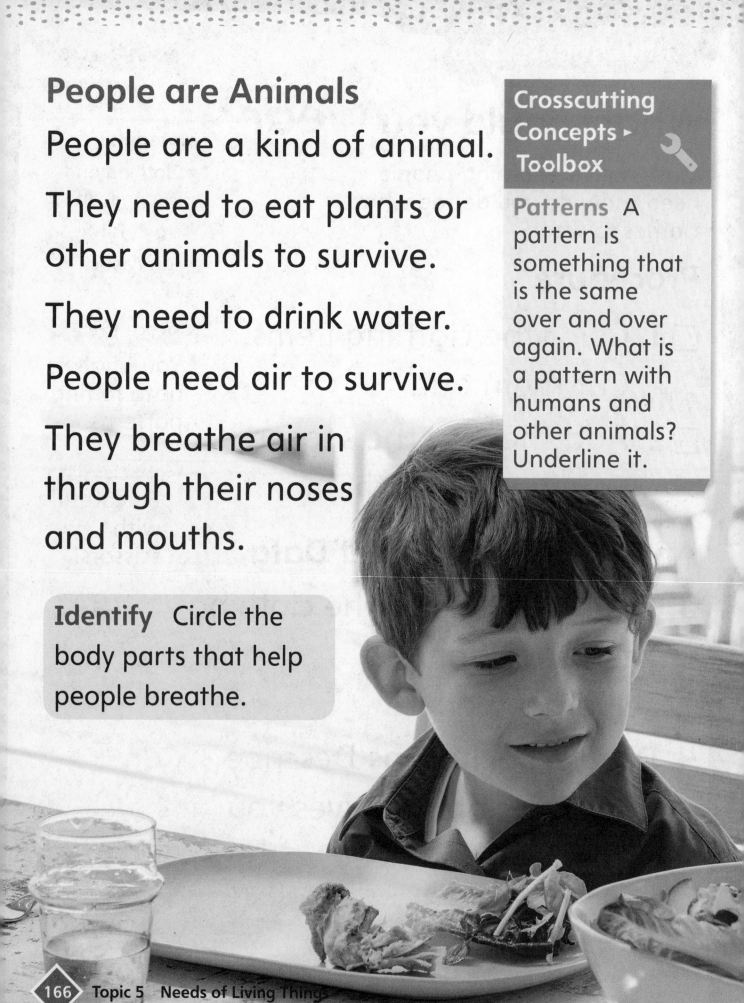

People are Animals

People are a kind of animal.

They need to eat plants or other animals to survive.

They need to drink water.

People need air to survive.

They breathe air in through their noses and mouths.

Identify Circle the body parts that help people breathe.

Crosscutting Concepts ▸ Toolbox

Patterns A pattern is something that is the same over and over again. What is a pattern with humans and other animals? Underline it.

People Need Clothes and Shelter

People wear clothes.

They use **shelters**.

Shelters are things that cover and protect.

Shelters keep people safe from the weather.

☑ **Reading Check** **Alike and Different** Underline two words that show how people are different from other animals.

Quest Connection

▼▼▼▼▼▼▼▼▼▼▼▼▼▼▼▼▼▼ ▼▼ ▼▼▼▼▼▼▼▼▼▼▼▼

Tell a partner something people need to spend a day in the park. Explain why people need it.

A Place to Sit

Shelters will be part of the park. Imagine it is a hot day.

Identify Circle items in the picture that will help people stay cool and dry on a hot day.

Hold It In!

The water-holding frog can live in the soil for two years without eating or drinking. When it rains, it takes water in through the skin. If you squeezed the water-holding frog, water would come out!

Infer How do water-holding frogs survive when it does not rain for a long time?

_____

_____

_____

_____

_____

Life Cycles

▶ VIDEO

Go online to learn more about the life cycle of a salmon.

Vocabulary

life cycle
change
hatch

I can understand how living things change as they go through life cycles.

K-LS1-1

Jumpstart Discovery!

Be a newborn bird coming out of an egg. Act it out.

How does a plant grOW and change?

How can you show how a plant grows?

Procedure

Materials
- potting soil
- clear plastic cups
- marigold seeds

☐ **1.** Tell what a plant needs to grow.

☐ **2.** Use the materials to grow a plant.

☐ **3. Observe** your plant each day. Draw pictures to show how it changes.

Science Practice

You **make observations** to answer science questions.

Day __	Day __	Day __

Analyze and Interpret Data

4. Describe Tell how the plant changes?

Living Things have Life Cycles

Living things go through different stages of life. These are called **life cycles**.

Change means to become different. All living things change during their life cycles.

When you were born, you were a little baby. Now, you are bigger.

> **Identify** Draw a circle on the first part of a life cycle.

Babies Look Different from their Parents

INTERACTIVITY

Go online to explore the life cycle of a pepper plant.

Many animals look different from their parents.

A newborn seal is white.

It changes color as it grows up.

☑ **Reading Check** **Alike and Different** Circle a word that shows how newborn seals are different from their parents.

Life Cycles Can Begin With Eggs

Some living things come from eggs.
Newborn birds **hatch**, or come out of, an egg.
A newborn penguin is gray and fuzzy when it hatches.
As it grows, its feathers will change.

A salamander lays eggs in water.
The young salamander looks very different from the adult.
It changes its shape as it grows.

adult penguins

adult salamander

Quest Connection

What do young penguins need to grow into adults?

Quest Check-In Lab

How do caterpillars change?

What does the town need to do if it wants to have butterflies?

Materials
- caterpillars
- sticks
- plants
- netted enclosure
- sugar water
- feeding pipette

Procedure

☐ **1.** Think about what caterpillars need.

☐ **2.** Use the materials. Make a plan to take care of the caterpillars.

Science Practice

You **observe** to find answers to science questions.

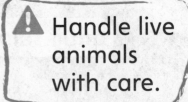

⚠ Handle live animals with care.

☐ **3.** Observe the caterpillars.
Draw what you see.

Day ____	Day ____	Day ____

Analyze and Interpret Data

4. What happened to the caterpillars?

_____

_____

_____

5. Identify What does the park need so
that it can have many butterflies?

_____

_____

_____

👆 **INTERACTIVITY**

Go online to learn more about what living things need.

Let's Build a Park!

What do plants and animals need to live in a park?

Phenomenon These plants and animals will live in the park. What will they need?

Show What You Found

Now, let's draw a picture of the park. You can draw the animals and the plants that will live there. Draw what they will need to survive.

Wildlife Biologist

Wildlife biologists study living things. They often work outdoors. They can travel to many places.

Where would you like to go if you were a wildlife biologist? Why?

_____

_____

_____

_____

_____

_____

The Essential Question
What do plants and animals need to survive?

Show What You Learned
Tell what you learned about plants and animals.

1. How does a plant get food?

    a. It makes its own food.

    b. It eats other plants.

    c. It eats animals.

    d. It makes sunlight.

2. What is one need cats and people share?

    a. They both need tools.

    b. They both need sunlight.

    c. They both need water.

    d. They both need clothes.

3. Compare what plants and animals need to survive. Use the word bank.

| water air sunlight food |

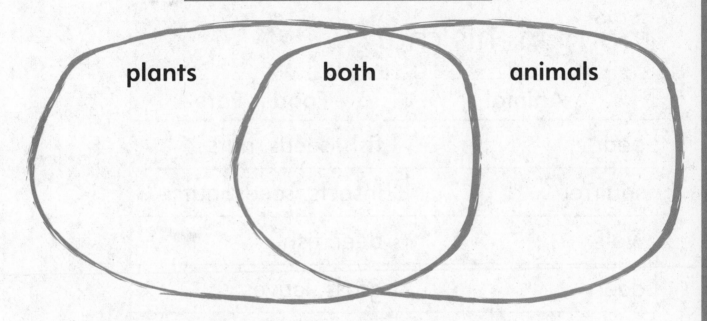

plants   both   animals

4. Put the life cycle of the plant in order. Use the numbers 1, 2, 3.

Read this scenario and answer the questions.

Nora did research about some animals. She wrote what she found in this chart.

Animal	Food it Eats
bear	fish, seeds, nuts
squirrel	insects, seeds, nuts
wolf	deer, fish
deer	grass, leaves

1. How do the animals get food?
   a. They use sunlight.
   b. They eat living things.
   c. They breathe it in.
   d. They find it in a store.

2. Decide if the statement is true or false. Put a check in the correct box.

	True	False
All animals eat plants.		
Animals make their own food.		
Some animals eat the same food.		

3. What might happen if a deer and a wolf meet?

_____

_____

_____

4. According to Nora's chart, which animal eats only plants?

a. bear

b. squirrel

c. wolf

d. deer

What needs do pets have?

Phenomenon You have learned that different animals have different needs. What are some needs that pets have?

Materials
- books about pets

You **observe** to find answers to questions.

Procedure

☐ **1.** Think of a pet you have or would like to have.

☐ **2.** Use the books to find what the pet needs.

☐ **3.** Record your data.
Follow the example.

Observations

Type of Pet	Food	Water	Shelter	Space
Snake	mice	bowl	rocks	fish tank

Analyze and Interpret Data

4. Compare Show your data to another group. How are the foods of the animals alike and different?

_____

_____

5. Identify What pattern do you see for the pets you studied?

_____

_____

Topic 6

Environments

Next Generation Science Standards

K-ESS2-2. Construct an argument supported by evidence for how plants and animals (including humans) can change the environment to meet their needs

K-ESS3-1 Use a model to represent the relationship between the needs of different plants or animals (including humans) and the places they live

K-ESS3-3. Communicate solutions that will reduce the impact of humans on the land, water, air, and/or other living things in the local environment

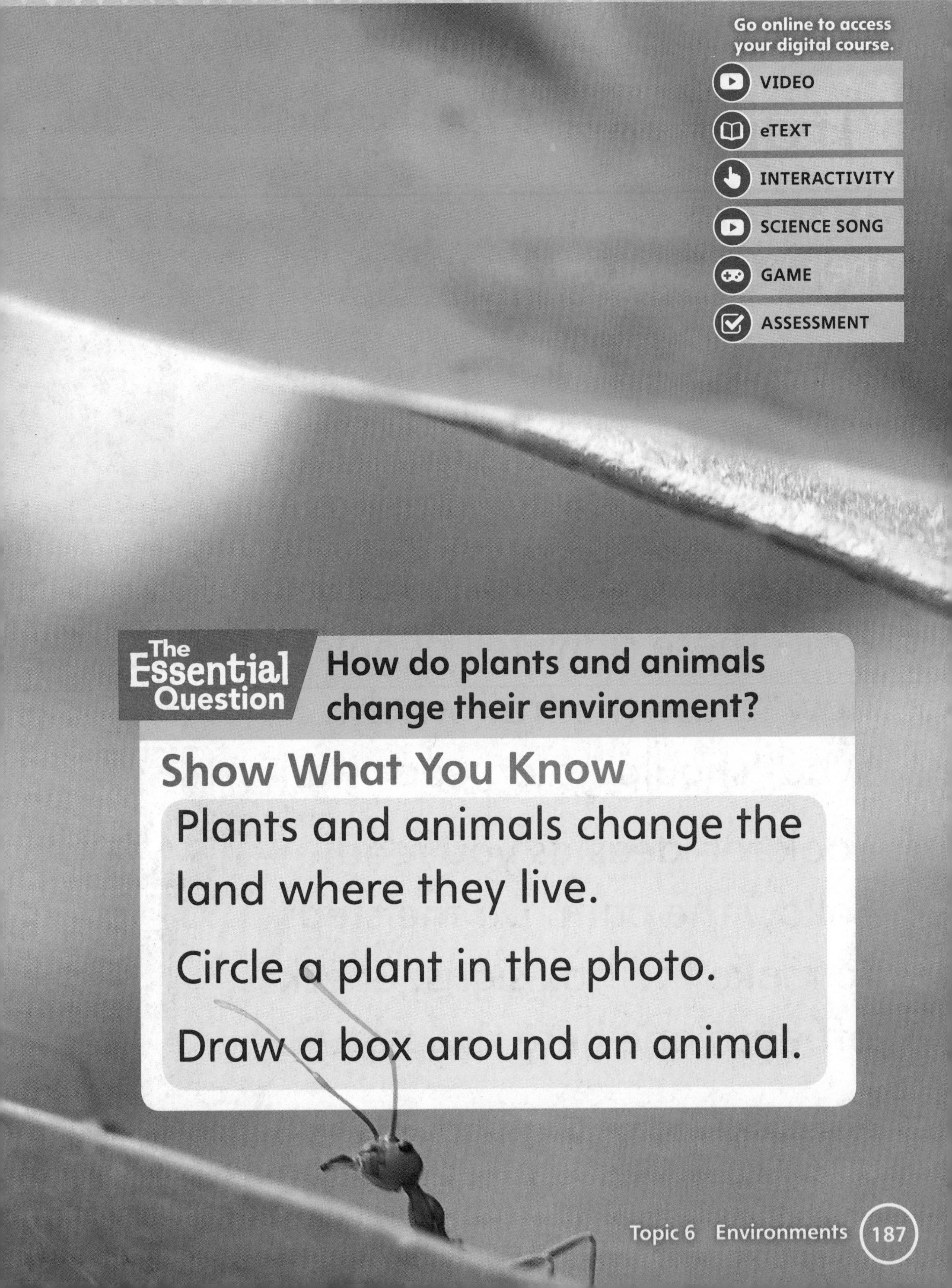

Go online to access
your digital course.

▶ VIDEO

📖 eTEXT

👆 INTERACTIVITY

▶ SCIENCE SONG

🎮 GAME

☑ ASSESSMENT

The Essential Question

How do plants and animals change their environment?

Show What You Know

Plants and animals change the land where they live.

Circle a plant in the photo.

Draw a box around an animal.

Trails for All

How do people change their local environment?

Phenomenon Hi, I'm Mr. Stone.

I'm a park ranger. I help people observe living things.

I have new signs for a nature trail. These signs tell people how to use the trail wisely. What should go on each sign?

Look for ideas as you read. Follow the path. Do the steps to make the trail signs. Check off each one here. QUEST CHECK ✓ OFF

Next Generation Science Standards

K-ESS2-2. Construct an argument supported by evidence for how plants and animals (including humans) can change the environment to meet their needs

K-ESS3-3. Communicate solutions that will reduce the impact of humans on the land, water, air, and/or other living things in the local environment

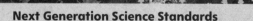

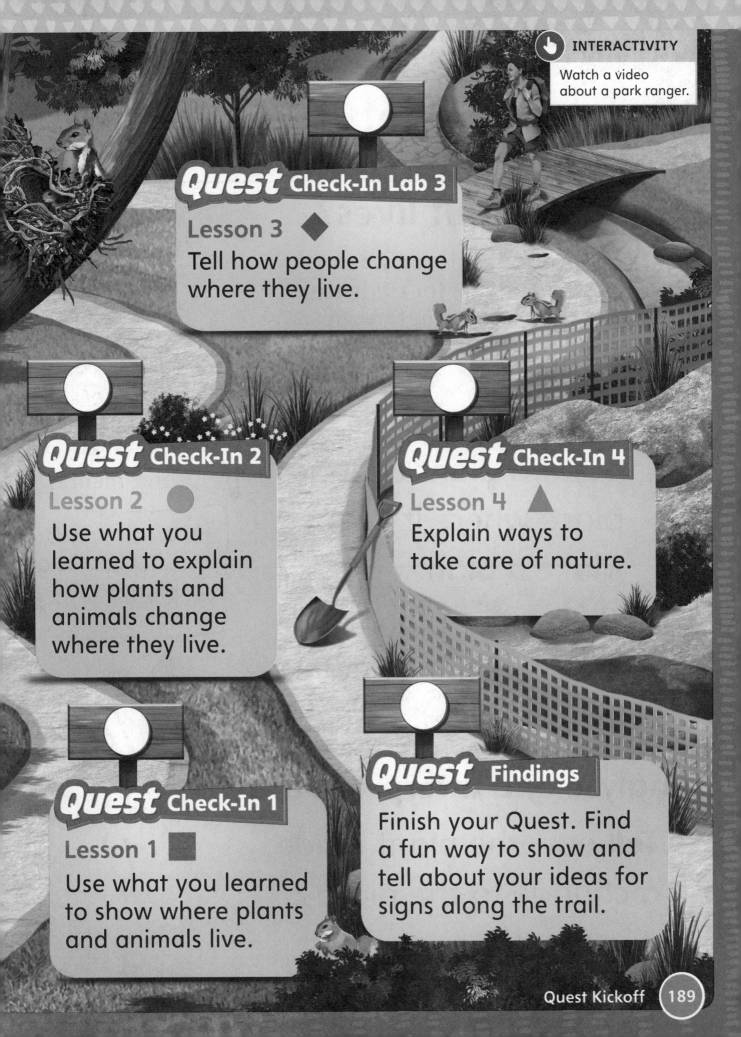

Quest Check-In Lab 3

Lesson 3 ◆
Tell how people change where they live.

Quest Check-In 2

Lesson 2 ●
Use what you learned to explain how plants and animals change where they live.

Quest Check-In 4

Lesson 4 ▲
Explain ways to take care of nature.

Quest Check-In 1

Lesson 1 ■
Use what you learned to show where plants and animals live.

Quest Findings
Finish your Quest. Find a fun way to show and tell about your ideas for signs along the trail.

How does a plant make a change to the place where it lives?

Scientists look for evidence when they investigate. Look for evidence to answer the question in the title.

Procedure

☐ **1.** Use the materials to find out if a plant changes the place where it lives. Make a plan.

☐ **2.** Show your plan to your teacher. Do your investigation.

Analyze and Interpret Data

3. Tell how the plant made a change to the place where it lives.

Material
- radish seeds
- clear plastic cups
- soil
- water

Science Practice

You use **evidence** to make an argument.

⚠ Wash hands after handling plants and soil.

Sequence

Scientists observe how animals change the places where they live.

How can a squirrel make a change?

 GAME

Practice what you learn with the Mini Games.

Sequence means to put things in order. "First," "next," and "last" are sequence words.

A Squirrel Hides Food

First, the squirrel digs a hole.

Next, it drops a nut into the hole.

Last, the animal covers the nut with dirt.

✓ **Reading Check**   **Sequence**

Circle what happens first.

Where Plants and Animals Live

▶ **VIDEO**

Watch a video about where plants and animals live.

Vocabulary

shelter

forest

plain

desert

ocean

I can observe different places where plants and animals live.

K-ESS3-1

Jumpstart Discovery!

Name a plant or animal that lives near you.

HANDS-ON LAB

K-ESS3-1, SEP.2

Who lives here?

Scientists make models to show where plants and animals live.

What plants and animals live near you?

Material
- crayons
- paper

Procedure

☐ 1. Think of plants and animals that live near you.

☐ 2. Draw a picture of the plants and animals that live near you.

Science Practice

When you draw, you make a **model**.

Analyze and Interpret Data

3. Tell a partner where your plants and animals live.

4. Explain why you think your drawing is a good model to show this place.

Needs

Plants and animals need water, air, and resources from the land.

Animals need air, food, and water.

Plants need air, water, and space to grow.

Animals need shelter. A **shelter** is a safe place to live.

Plants and animals live where they can survive.

Sequence Look at the three pictures. What is the first step in building a bird nest? Put a box around the photo.

Forests and Plains

Some plants and animals live in forests.

A **forest** is land with many trees.

Some plants and animals live on the plains.

A **plain** is a flat area of land with lots of grass.

_____

_____

Label Write a label for each photo.

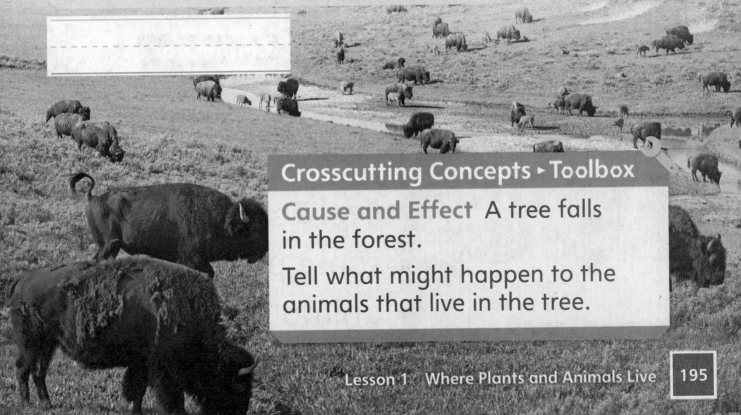

_____

Crosscutting Concepts ▸ Toolbox

Cause and Effect A tree falls in the forest.

Tell what might happen to the animals that live in the tree.

Deserts and Oceans

INTERACTIVITY
Learn more about a desert environment.

Some plants and animals live in the desert.

A **desert** is very dry land.

Some plants and animals live in the ocean.

The **ocean** is a big area of salt water.

_____

Label Write a label for each photo.

_____

Quest Connection

Tell about some places where plants live. Tell about some places where animals find shelter.

A Nature Walk

People like to hike in nature.

People like to go on trails.

People like to see plants and animals where they live.

Draw Make a trail sign to protect living things by telling people where the plants and animals live.

Plants and Animals Change the Environment

▶ **VIDEO**

Watch a video about how plants and animals change their environment.

Vocabulary

environment

I can observe ways that plants and animals change their environment.

KESS2-2 K-ESS3-1

Jumpstart Discovery!

Look at the picture.

How are plants, animals, and people making changes?

Circle four ways.

How do squirrels change the land?

Scientists use evidence to support their opinions. How can you use a model to get evidence?

Procedure

☐ 1. Show ways that squirrels can change the land.

☐ 2. Build your model and then draw it.

Materials

- container of damp sand
- classroom objects to represent nuts, acorns, and seeds

Science Practice

You can use **evidence** to support your argument.

Analyze and Interpret Data

3. **Tell** how your model shows that squirrels change the land. Use evidence.

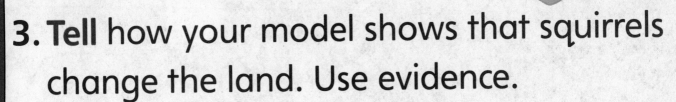

Where Plants Live

A plant is part of its **environment**. An environment is everything around a living thing.

A plant can change its environment.

INTERACTIVITY

Show how plants and animals change their environment.

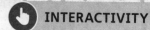

Sequence Tell what happens first, next, and last. Write 1, 2, or 3 in each box.

Quest Connection

Tell how a plant can change its environment.

Animals in Their Environment

An animal can change its environment.

Termites make huge nests.

Elk eat grass and flowers.

Describe Tell about another animal that can change its environment.

termites and nest

elk eating grass

Plants and Animals Together

Plants and animals live together in an environment.

Animals help plants by spreading their seeds.

Plants help animals by providing food and shelter.

Systems When plants and animals live and work together, that is called a system. Tell what would happen to the animals that eat grass if all the grass died.

Identify Look at the photos. Tell how the plants and animals live together.

Changes in Nature

Plants and animals can change their environments. Plants and animals can change how a trail looks. Look at the photos that show changes.

Draw Make a trail sign to tell how the plants and animals in the pictures changed the nature trail.

People Change the Environment

▶ VIDEO

Watch a video about how people change their environment.

Vocabulary
resources

I can observe ways that people change their environment.

K-ESS3-1 K-ESS2-2 K-ESS3-3

Jumpstart Discovery!

You want to make a garden. Name the tools you will use. Act out how to use each tool.

How can you model changing the environment?

Workers changed the land to build your school.

How can you make a model to show other changes?

Procedure

☐ 1. Make a model of land.

☐ 2. Find ways to make changes to your model.

Analyze and Interpret Data

3. **Explain** What is the biggest change you made?

_____

- - - - - - - - - - - - - - - - -

_____

4. **Draw Conclusions** Tell how people changed the land near where you live.

Materials
- container of sand or dirt
- water

Suggested Materials
- toy garden tools
- toy construction vehicles

Science Practice

You use a **model** to answer questions about nature.

People and Resources

Resources are things that people use to live.

Air, soil, water, and plants are some resources. People need resources.

cutting down a tree

wood from trees

fresh water

Getting What We Need

INTERACTIVITY

Learn more about how people change their environment.

People change the environment to get the resources they need.

Sometimes the changes can hurt the land, soil, air, or water.

stream with trash

Identify Look at the photos. Tell one way to stop changes that hurt the land, air, soil, and water.

Quest Connection

Tell how people changed the environment.

How can people change the land?

Park rangers make sure the trail is not being damaged by too many people using it.

What happens to the plants if a trail is used too much?

Materials

- container of sand or dirt
- toy people
- model trees, plants, or bushes

Science Practice

A **model** can help you understand events.

Procedure

☐ 1. Make a model of a trail.

☐ 2. Find ways to show what happens when many people use the trail.

Analyze and Interpret Data

3. **Explain** How do the people and plants change the trail?

4. **Describe** Tell how the plants look different.

Subtracting Numbers

Subtracting is taking one number away from another to tell how many.

Look at the picture on the left.

Write how many trees there are.

Look at the picture on the right.

Write how many trees there are.

Left _____ **trees**   **Right** _____ **trees**

Complete the subtraction problem.

_____ **trees** – _____ **trees** = _____ **trees**

Lesson 4

People Can Protect the Environment

▶ VIDEO

Watch a video about how people can protect their environment.

Vocabulary

recycle

reuse

I can tell how **I can** protect the environment.

K-ESS2-2, K-ESS3-3

Jumpstart Discovery!

Tell one way that you can help the environment.

How can you make something useful?

We throw away many things that we can use again. How can you make something useful from something old?

Design and Make It!

☐ **1.** Choose something old.

☐ **2.** Think of ways to change it to make something useful.

☐ **3.** Ask your teacher for help if you need it.

☐ **4.** Make something useful.

Evaluate Your Design

5. Tell how people can use the object you made.

Suggested Materials

• old, clean socks

• clean cans, plastic bottles and jars

• paper and fabric scraps

• safety scissors

• glue

Engineering Practice

You can **design** a solution to a problem.

 Be careful with scissors.

New Uses for Old Things

INTERACTIVITY

Show how you can protect Earth.

People can help Earth.

We can reuse objects.

Reuse means we can use an object again.

Quest Connection

Tell how reusing and recycling helps the environment.

Helping Earth

People can recycle things.

Recycle means we can make an object into something new.

We can recycle bottles and cans.

We can recycle paper and cloth.

Explain Write a caption for the photo of the bins.

_____

_____

_____

Crosscutting Concepts ▸ Toolbox

Cause and Effect
Look at the photo of trash. Tell what caused this to happen.

What You Can Do

We all need to protect the environment.

You can use less water.

You can reuse things you have.

Draw a way you help Earth.

Stay on a bike path.

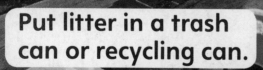

Put litter in a trash can or recycling can.

Turn off the water while you brush your teeth.

Help other people reuse.

DONATION

Crosscutting Concepts ▸ Toolbox

Systems in Our World Tell how you can protect the air and water you need.

Pick up litter when you see it.

How can we save our trails?

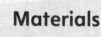

Some people ride bikes on nature trails.

Some people walk on nature trails.

What happens when too many people and bikes use nature trails?

Materials
- model from Lesson 3
- craft sticks
- tape
- model plants
- markers

Model

☐ **1.** Look at each picture. Think about what each picture is showing.

☐ **2.** Choose one picture.

☐ **3.** Use your model from Lesson 3.

Engineering Practice

You can **design a solution** to a problem.

☐ **4.** Use your model to show how to save the trail.

☐ **5.** Make a sign that will help save the trail. Put it with your model.

Draw your model and sign

Evaluate Your Model

6. Explain your solution to a partner.

K-2-ETS1-1

INTERACTIVITY

Watch a video about how engineers use tools.

The Problem with a Tree

Phenomenon Jay and his dad built a tree house.

How can Jay get up in the tree?

Design It

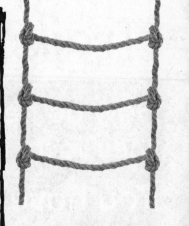

- ☐ What is the problem?

  _____

  - - - - - - - - - - - - - - - - -

  _____

- ☐ Look at the clues.

- ☐ Draw two new ideas that Jay could try.

- ☐ Talk with a partner. Choose the best idea.

Trails for All

How do people change their local environment?

You have learned how people can change an environment.

Show What You Found

Phenomenon You have made some trail signs to protect a nature trail.

What other signs can you make to help the park ranger save the nature trails?

Tell how your signs will help plants and animals on the trail.

Park Ranger

Park rangers keep parks safe for animals, plants, and people.

A ranger shows people how plants and animals live together in an environment.

Would you like to be a park ranger?

Explain in a sentence.

_____

_____

_____

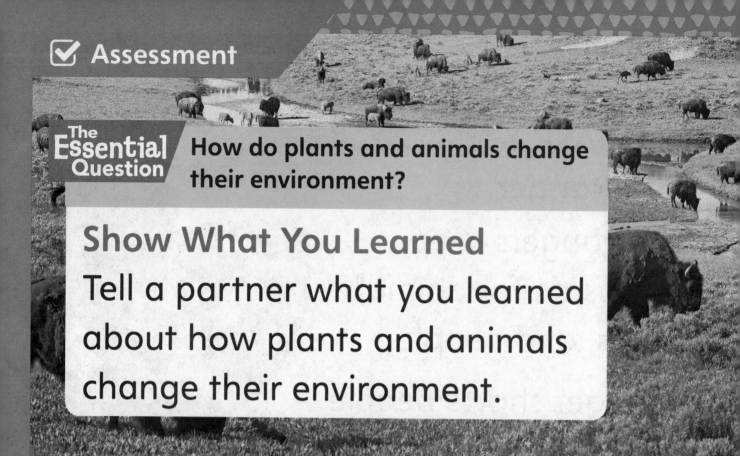

The Essential Question
How do plants and animals change their environment?

Show What You Learned
Tell a partner what you learned about how plants and animals change their environment.

1. Choose a word from the word bank to correctly complete the sentence. The photo shows a animal in the

_____

- - - - - - - - - - - - - - -

_____ .

| desert | forest | plain | ocean |

2. What is an environment?

   a. a way to reuse objects in the trash

   b. everything around a living thing

   c. an animal that can meet its needs

   d. a plant that can meet its needs

3. Why should people recycle?

   a. to use more resources

   b. to keep plants and animals safe

   c. to get more sun and water

   d. to use fewer resources.

4. What is one way you can help Earth?

   a. Go to the store every day.

   b. Turn on the lights at home.

   c. Reuse toys and books.

   d. Eat more fish and meat.

Read and answer questions 1-4.

Ella loves to camp. Her family likes to camp by Elk River. But this year, something has changed. Use the pictures to answer the questions.

1. What kind of environment does Ella camp in?

a. an ocean

b. a plain

c. a desert

d. a forest

2. How did the environment change?

   a. Trees were cut down.

   b. Animals made homes in the soil.

   c. Trees fell over in a storm.

   d. Campers caught too many fish.

3. Why did the change happen?

   a. to meet animals' needs

   b. to meet people's needs

   c. to help plants grow bigger
      and stronger

   d. to give fish a better home

4. Tell how the environment
   can be protected.

   _____

   _____

   _____

   _____

How can an animal change where it lives?

Materials
- worms
- soil
- clear plastic container with lid
- gloves
- black paper
- tape

Phenomenon Scientists observe with their senses. How do worms change the soil where they live?

Procedure

- ☐ **1.** Make a plan to show how worms change soil.

- ☐ **2.** Show your plan to your teacher.

- ☐ **3.** Observe the worms for 5 days.

- ☐ **4.** Draw your observations on Day 1.

Science Practice

You use **evidence** to make an argument.

⚠ Wear gloves when handling worms.

How Worms Change Soil Day 1

☐ **5.** Draw your observations on Day 5.

How Worms Change Soil Day 5

Analyze and Interpret Data

6. Explain how worms changed their environment. Use your drawings as evidence.

Science and Engineering Practices Handbook

Science Practices

Questions

Scientists ask questions about the world.

They might ask, "What do plants need?"

Then scientists do tests to find answers.

These tests are called experiments.

Ask a question about plants.

Scientists investigate plants.

SEP.1 Asking questions and defining problems
SEP.3 Planning and carrying out investigations

Scientists investigate to look for answers.

They only investigate one thing at a time.

This is called a fair test.

Look at this investigation of plants and water.

This plant got little water.

Scientists gave this plant a lot of water.

Tell whether this is a fair test. Why or why not?

Science Practices

Observations

You observe when you pay close attention to things.

Scientists use their senses to observe.

They record observations.

They can draw or write what they observe.

flowering plant

Observe the plant.
Record your observations.

What do you observe?	Information
Number of leaves	
Color of flower petals	

Data

Data are information.

Scientists collect data from observations.

Data may tell what something looks and feels like.

Scientists share data with others.

Turn to a partner.
Share data about yourself!

Science Practices

Tools

Scientists use tools to collect information.

They can use a magnifying glass to see small things.

They can use a thermometer to tell how hot or cold something is.

They can use a ruler to find out how big something is.

Circle a tool you can use to see things.

Measure

You can collect data by measuring.

Metric rulers measure length.

A clock is used to measure time.

Length and weight are data.

Look around the room. Draw things that help you collect and record data.

Science Practices

Explanations

Scientists use models to explain how things work.

A model can be a drawing or a diagram.

You can also build a model.

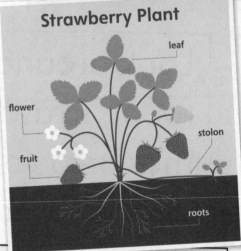

Strawberry Plant

leaf

flower

fruit

stolon

roots

Observe a plant. Draw a model of it. Tell how your model and the plant are alike and different.

SEP.2 Developing and using models
SEP.6 Constructing explanations and designing solutions
SEP.7 Engaging in argument from evidence

Evidence

Scientists also use evidence.

Facts and information are evidence.

Scientists get evidence from observations and data.

They use evidence to help their explanations.

Tell what evidence you see that caterpillars have been eating the leaves.

Science Practices

Teamwork

Scientists work with each other.

They share creative ideas.

They study the work of other scientists.

Then, they tell them what they think.

Tell a partner one thing you like about the plant model that they drew. Tell one thing they could add to their model.

Communication

Scientists communicate results.

You communicate when you share what you know.

Scientists publish their ideas.

Scientists learn from those ideas.

Communication helps all scientists.

As a class, decide what else you would like to know about plants. Write your question.

_____

_____

Tell where you could go to find the answer.

Engineering Practices

→ ## Define a Problem

Engineers define problems.

They choose goals to make things better.

→ ## Design a Solution

Engineers solve problems.

They think about materials that they can use.

Some engineers test models.

Look at the picture. Tell what problem you think this tool might solve.

SEP.1 Asking questions and defining problems
SEP.2 Developing and using models
SEP.3 Planning and carrying out investigations
SEP.4 Analyzing and interpreting data
SEP.6 Constructing explanations and designing solutions
SEP.7 Engaging in argument from evidence

Improve the Design

Engineers test their solutions.

They collect and record data to see how each solution works.

They share their solution.

Then they make improvements.

You improve something when you make it better.

Draw a picture that shows how you could make the tool even better.

Credits

Illustrations

Peter Bull Art Studio; Sara Lynn Cramb/Astound US; Peter Francis/MB Artists, Inc.; Lauren Gallegos/C.A. Tugeau, LLC; Patrick Gnan/IllustrationOnline.com; Bob Kayganich/IllustrationOnline.com; Kristen Kest/MB Artists, Inc.; Erika LeBarre/IllustrationOnline.com; Matt LeBarre/Blasco Creative, LLC; Lisa Manuzak/Astound; Precision Graphics/Lachina Publishing Services; Geoffrey P Smith; Jamie Smith/MB Artists, Inc.; Mark Rogalski/Painted Words, Inc.; Mike Rothman/Melissa Turk; Ralph Voltz/IllustrationOnline.com

Photographs

Photo locators denoted as follows: Top (T), Center (C), Bottom (B), Left (L), Right (R), Background (Bkgd)

Covers

Front Cover: Mikkel Bigandt/Shutterstock; Back Cover: Marinello/DigitalVision Vectors/Getty Images.

Front Matter

iv: Clari Massimiliano/Shutterstock; vi: Andresr/Shutterstock; vii: Cheryl Savan/Shutterstock; viii: Stephen Coburn/Shutterstock; ix: Andresr/Shutterstock; x: B.O'Kane/Alamy Stock Photo; xi: Franckreporter/Getty Images; xii Bkgrd: Brian J. Skerry/National Geographic/Getty Images; xii TR: Old Apple/Shutterstock; xiii B: Pearson Education; xiii TL: Pearson Education

Topic 1

000: F1online digitale Bildagentur GmbH/Alamy Stock Photo; 002 BR: John Davidson Photos/Alamy Stock Photo; 002 CR: Ben Welsh Premium/Alamy Stock Photo; 002 TCR: Kim Reinick/Shutterstock; 002 TR: Andresr/Shutterstock; 005: Michael Ireland/Fotolia; 006: Alexei_tm/Fotolia; 007 BCR: Nikshor/Shutterstock; 007 CR: Dima Sobko/ Shutterstock; 008: Cultura Creative (RF)/Alamy Stock Photo; 009: Andresr/Shutterstock; 010 BL: 2xSamara/Shutterstock; 010 BR: Jade Albert/Getty Images; 011: Andresr/Shutterstock; 014 Bkgrd: Trong Nguyen/Shutterstock; 014 BL: Sergey Novikov/Shutterstock; 015 BR: Pressmaster/Shutterstock; 015 C: Sergey Lavrentev/Shutterstock; 016: Andresr/Shutterstock; 018: Jenseman04/Fotolia; 022: Andraž Cerar/Shutterstock; 023 BL: Photodisc/Getty Images; 023 BR: Andresr/Shutterstock; 023 CR: Stephanie Swartz/Shutterstock; 028 Bkgrd: Go2dim/Fotolia; 028 BR: Andresr/Shutterstock; 028 C: Ben Welsh Premium/Alamy Stock Photo; 028 CL: Kim Reinick/Shutterstock; 028 CR: John Davidson Photos/Alamy Stock Photo; 028 TR: Scottish Viewpoint/Alamy Stock Photo; 029 Bkgrd: Michael Pole/Corbis RF Stills/Getty Images; 029 TR: Onne van der Wal/Corbis Documentary/Getty Images; 030 BR: Natalia Zhurbina/Shutterstock; 030 CR: Blend Images BUILT Content/Alamy Stock Photo; 030 T: Oticki/123RF; 030 TCR: Krishna Utkarsh Pandit/Shutterstock; 031: Denise Kappa/Shutterstock; 034 BC: Terekhov igor/Shutterstock; 034 BCR: Oez/Shutterstock; 034 BR: Airobody/Fotolia

Topic 2

036: Patrick Foto/Shutterstock; 037 BC: Sedlacekjan97/Fotolia; 037 Bkgrd: Calek/Shutterstock; 037 BL: Alexander Tarassov/Fotolia; 037 BR: Arina Zaiachin/123RF; 037 CR: Piikcoro/Shutterstock; 038: Cheryl Savan/Shutterstock; 040: Silkstock/Fotolia; 041: Lodimup/Fotolia; 042: Nataly Lukhanina/Shutterstock; 043: Sheva_ua/Fotolia; 044 B: Elena Yakusheva/Shutterstock; 044 C: Cheryl Savan/Shutterstock; 045 BR: Juriah Mosin/Shutterstock; 045 CL: Tom Wang/123RF; 045 CR: RooM the Agency/Alamy Stock Photo; 045 T: Jacek Chabraszewski/Shutterstock; 046: Olesya Feketa/Shutterstock; 047 BL: Trinacria Photo/Shutterstock; 047 BR: Petr Vaclavek/Shutterstock; 047 CL: Vladvm/Shutterstock; 047 CR: Thomas Brain/Shutterstock; 047 TCL: Keith Bell/Shutterstock; 047 TCR: Narith Thongphasuk/Shutterstock; 047 TL: Cheryl Savan/Shutterstock; 048: Dave King/DKImages; 049: Dave King/DKImages; 050 B: Baloncici/Shutterstock; 050 BR: IPostnikov/Shutterstock; 050 TR: Igor Negovelov/Fotolia; 051 BR: Cheryl Savan/Shutterstock; 051 TCR: Aldegonde/Shutterstock; 051 TL: Kristina Postnikova/Shutterstock; 051 TR: Lucie Zapletalova/Shutterstock; 053 Bkgrd: Oleandra/123RF; 053 BL: Jenifoto/Fotolia; 053 BR: Eskay Lim/Fotolia; 053 CR: Seramo/Shutterstock; 054: Cheryl Savan/Shutterstock; 055 B: Elisabeth Burrell/Alamy Stock Photo; 055 C: Picsfive/Shutterstock; 055 T: Ivonne Wierink/Fotolia; 057: Michael Nivelet/Shutterstock; 058: Cheryl Savan/Shutterstock; 059 B: Springfield Gallery/Fotolia; 059 TR: Image Source/Getty Images; 060 BR: Denis Kovin/Shutterstock; 060 TC: Cheryl Savan/Shutterstock; 061: akekoksomshutter/Shutterstock; 062: Zoonar GmbH/Alamy Stock Photo; 064 Bkgrd: Beloborod/Shutterstock; 064 C: Cheryl Savan/Shutterstock; 065 Bkgrd: iPostnikov/Shuttesrtock; 065 TR: FatCamera/Getty Images; 066: Andreas Kraus/Shutterstock; 067 BC: Sakdinon Kadchlangsaen/Shutterstock; 067 C: Ilya Andriyanov/Shutterstock; 067 CR: Nata777_7/Fotolia; 067 T: Dani Simmonds/Fotolia; 067 TCL: Jackhollingsworth/Shutterstock; 067 TR: Sumroeng Chinnapan/Shutterstock; 071 BC: Creative Crop/Getty Images; 071 BL: Tatiana Popova/Shutterstock; 071 BR: Triin Lakspere/Shutterstock

Topic 3

072: Connect11/iStock/Getty Images Plus/Getty Images; 074 BC: Jonathan Irish/National Geographic Magazines/Getty Images; 074 BL: Lurii/iStock/Getty Images Plus/Getty Images; 074 BR: P. Eoche/The Image Bank/Getty Images; 074 TR: Stephen Coburn/Shutterstock; 077 Bkgrd: Cultura Exclusive/Philip Lee Harvey/Cultura/Getty Images; 077 TR: Nature Photographers Ltd/Alamy Stock Photo; 078: Pavel_Klimenko/Shutterstock; 080: Marco Wong/Moment/Getty Images; 081: Stephen Coburn/Shutterstock; 082: Stephen Coburn/Shutterstock; 083 Bkgrd: Mrtomuk/iStock/Getty Images; 083 TR: B.A.E. Inc./Alamy Stock Photo; 084: Skynesher/E+/Getty Images; 087 BL: Xpixel/Shutterstock; 087 TC: Coprid/Shutterstock; 088: Jürgen Fälchle/Alamy Stock Photo; 090: Alina Pavlova/Alamy Stock Photo; 091 B: AlinaMD/iStock/Getty Images; 091 CR: Stephen Coburn/Shutterstock; 091 T: Kryuchka Yaroslav/Shutterstock; 092 BR: 123RF; 092 TR: Stephen Coburn/Shutterstock; 093: Aopsan/Shutterstock; 094 Bkgrd: Alex Kosev/Shutterstock; 094 BR: Stephen Coburn/Shutterstock; 095 Bkgrd: Sylv1rob1/Shutterstock; 095 TR: Vgajic/E+/Getty Images; 096: AlinaMD/Shutterstock; 100: TerryM/Shutterstock

Topic 4

102: Boon/Getty Images; 104: Andresr/Shutterstock; 106: Photolinc/Shutterstock; 107: Skreidzeleu/Shutterstock; 108: Tim Gainey/Alamy Stock Photo; 109: Patpitchaya/Shutterstock; 110 BL: Stephanie Rausser/Getty Images; 110 R: Appletat/iStock/Getty Images; 111 BC: Andresr/Shutterstock; 111 BR: andreiuc88/Shutterstock; 111 CR: Will Blaik/EyeEm/Getty Images; 111 TR: Vibrant Image Studio/Shutterstock; 112 B: Lester Balajadia/Shutterstock; 112 CR: George W. Bailey/Shutterstock; 113 BC: andreiuc88/Shutterstock; 113 BL: HorenkO/Shutterstock; 113 BR: Janis Smits/Shutterstock; 113 TL: Andresr/Shutterstock; 114: Jordan Siemens/Digital Vision/Getty Images; 116: Igor Goncharenko/Alamy Stock Photo; 117: NilsJohan Norenlind/Getty Images; 118 Bkgrd: Elenamiv/Shutterstock; 118 R: Nidwlw/Getty Images; 119 BL: Russ Rohde/CulturaRF/Getty Images; 119 BR: Andresr/Shutterstock; 119 C: BJI/Blue Jean Images/Getty Images; 119 TR: YanLev/Shutterstock; 120 Bkgrd: BSIP SA/Alamy Stock Photo; 120 TR: Michele Oenbrink/Alamy; 121: Andresr/Shutterstock; 122: Image Source/Alamy Stock Photo; 124: HannamariaH/Getty Images; 125 CR: Andresr/Shutterstock; 126 B: dolennen/Shutterstock; 127: Sergey Novikov/Alamy Stock Photo; 128: Paul Avis/Getty Images; 130 Bkgrd: Jason Persoff Stormdoctor/Getty Images; 130 TR: Todd Shoemake/Shutterstock; 131 Bkgrd: Mike Hill/Alamy Stock Photo; 131 BR: Andresr/Shutterstock; 132 B: Krisana Tongnantree/Shutterstock; 132 TR: Dana Hoff/Corbis/Getty Images; 133 B: Science Photo Library/NOAA/Getty Images; 133 CR: Chesky/Shutterstock; 134 BR: Andersphoto/Shutterstock; 134 TC: Andresr/Shutterstock; 136 Bkgrd: Pictureguy/Shutterstock; 136 BR: Andresr/Shutterstock; 137 Bkgrd: Ryan K. McGinnis/Alamy Stock Photo; 137 TR: Ryan K. McGinnis/Alamy Stock Photo; 138: Rob Hainer/Shutterstock; 139: Nidwlw/Getty Images; 140: Nidwlw/Getty Images

Topic 5

144: Elusive Photography/Getty Images; 146: B.O'Kane/Alamy Stock Photo; 148 BR: Khak/Shutterstock; 148 CR: Kirillov alexey/Shutterstock; 149 B: Pascal Janssen/Shutterstock; 149 TR: Yykkaa/Getty Images; 150: Djgis/Shutterstock; 152: Blickwinkel/Alamy Stock Photo; 154 BL: Sundraw Photography/Shutterstock; 154 BR: B.O'Kane/Alamy Stock Photo; 154 CR: Cultura Creative/Alamy Stock Photo; 155 BL: Topnatthapon/Shutterstock; 155 BR: A454/iStock/Getty Images; 155 CL: Pakhnyushchy/Shutterstock; 155 CR: Viewin/Shutterstock; 155 TL: B.O'Kane/Alamy Stock Photo; 156: National Geographic Creative/Alamy Stock Photo; 158 Bkgrd: Dmitry Pichugin/Shutterstock; 158 BR: Adriana Margarita Larios Arellano/Shutterstock; 158 BR: Kamenetskiy Konstantin/Shutterstock; 158 CL: Marevision/Getty Images; 158 CR: KAMONRAT/Shutterstock; 158 TC: Aksenova Natalya/Shutterstock; 159: B.O'Kane/Alamy Stock Photo; 160 B: Alexey Stiop/Alamy Stock Photo; 160 TR: Fox_krol/Shutterstock; 161 Bkgrd: BasieB/Getty Images; 161 TL: B.O'Kane/Alamy Stock Photo; 162: 3dfoto/Shutterstock; 164: Imgorthand/Getty Images; 166: Eric Audras/Getty Images; 167 BC: B.O'Kane/Alamy Stock Photo; 167 TR: FamVeld/Shutterstock; 168 B: Francesco Scatena/Shutterstock; 168 C: Barrett & MacKay/Getty Images; 168 TL: B.O'Kane/Alamy Stock Photo; 169 Bkgrd: Uwe Bergwitz/Shutterstock; 169 CR: Wayne G. Lawler/Science Source; 169 TR: B.G. Thomson/Science Source; 172 BC: Monkey Business Images/Shutterstock; 172 BL: 2p2play/Shutterstock; 172 BR: Leungchopan/Shutterstock; 173 Bkgrd: Johnny Johnson/Getty Images; 173 CR: ImageBROKER/Alamy Stock Photo; 174 BCR: Lisad1724/iStock/Getty Images; 174 BR: Matt Jeppson./Shutterstock; 174 TCR: Anthony Lister/123RF; 174 TR: Wildscotphotos/Alamy Stock Photo; 175 B: Robert HENNO/Alamy Stock Photo; 175 BR: B.O'Kane/Alamy Stock Photo; 175 T: All Canada Photos/Alamy Stock Photo; 176 BL: Andrew Waugh/Alamy Stock Photo; 176 C: B.O'Kane/Alamy Stock Photo; 177: AlasdairJames/iStock/Getty Images; 178 Bkgrd: Sevenke/Shutterstock; 178 BR: B.O'Kane/Alamy Stock Photo; 178 C: Adriana Margarita Larios Arellano/Shutterstock; 178 CL: Ivonne Wierink/Shutterstock; 178 CR: Steve Bylan/Shutterstock; 179 Bkgrd: Aurora Photos/Alamy Stock Photo; 179 TR: WAYHOME studio/Shutterstock; 180: Mashabuba/Getty Images; 181 BC: Malgorzata Slusarczyk/123RF; 181 BL: Golfx/Shutterstock; 181 BR: Karen Winton/Shutterstock; 184: Chaistock/Shutterstock

Topic 6

186: Andrew JK Tan/Getty Images; 188 BR: Ahturner/Shutterstock; 188 CR: Tom Uhlman/Alamy Stock Photo; 188 TR: Franckreporter/Getty Images; 190: Abramova Elena/Shutterstock; 191: Alexandra Giese/Shutterstock; 192: Robert Bohrer/Shutterstock; 193: Pixeljoy/Shutterstock; 194 BR: Anthony Ricci/Shutterstock; 194 CR: Stone Nature Photography/Alamy Stock Photo; 194 TR: Kevin E. Beasley/Shutterstock; 195 B: Betty4240/iStock/Getty Images; 195 TR: Erik Mandre/Shutterstock; 196 B: Brandon Rosenblum/Getty Images; 196 BR: Franckreporter/Getty Images; 196 TR: Luke Wait/Shutterstock; 197 Bkgrd: William Silver/Shutterstock; 197 TL: Franckreporter/Getty Images; 200 BC: Franckreporter/Getty Images; 200 Bkgrd: Salajean/Shutterstock; 201 Bkgrd: Design Pics Inc/Alamy Stock Photo; 201 CR: Brandon Rosenblum/Getty Images; 201 TR: Auscape/UIG/Getty Images; 202 B: Kaichankava Larysa/Shutterstock; 202 TR: Non15/Shutterstock; 203 B: S.Z./Shutterstock; 203 TL: Franckreporter/Getty Images; 203 TR: FloridaStock/Shutterstock; 204: Mint Images/Michael Hanson/Getty Images; 205: Noam Armonn/Shutterstock; 206 Bkgrd: George Rath Jr./Shutterstock; 206 CL: Elena Elisseeva/Shutterstock; 206 CR: Smereka/Shutterstock; 206 TR: Dmitry Kalinovsky/Shutterstock; 207 B: Ivan Sabo/Shutterstock; 207 BR: Franckreporter/Getty Images; 207 TR: David W. Leindecker/Shutterstock; 208 BR: 2009fotofriends/Shutterstock; 208 TC: Franckreporter/Getty Images; 210: JBryson/iStock/Getty Images; 212 BC: Franckreporter/Getty Images; 212 Bkgrd: Lamyai/Shutterstock; 212 TR: Extradeda/Shutterstock; 213 B: ZQFotography/Shutterstock; 213 CR: Huguette Roe/Shutterstock; 214 B: Tony Freeman/Photo Edit; 214 TR: JaySi/Shutterstock; 215 BR: Fuse/Corbis/Getty Images; 215 CR: Adriaticfoto/Shutterstock; 215 TR: Sam BloombergRissman/Eddy Joaquim/Getty Images; 216 BL: ATJA/Shutterstock; 216 BR: R A Kearton/Getty Images; 216 CR: Graham Taylor Photography/Shutterstock; 216 TR: Franckreporter/Getty Images; 218: Sashk0/Shutterstock; 219 BR: Grynold/Shutterstock; 219 CR: Andrii Gorulko/Shutterstock; 219 TCR: Kotema/Shutterstock; 219 TR: SeDmi/Shutterstock; 220 Bkgrd: Gerald A. DeBoer/Shutterstock; 220 C: Franckreporter/Getty Images; 221 Bkgrd: John Lund/Sam Diephuis/Getty Images; 221 TR: Blend Images/Alamy Stock Photo; 222 BR: Dmodlin01/

Credits